Japanese Religion

James M. Vardaman

Sawada Gumi

装　　幀 = 寄藤文平、福田　翼

本文イラスト = テッド高橋

日本語校閲 = 吉田意弘

Proof-reading = Michael Brase

写真協力 = 中田 昭・塚田満雄・松岡徳昌・菱木啓美
　　　　　「photolibrary」web サイト　http://www.photolibrary.jp/
　　　　　「写真素材足成」web サイト　http://www.ashinari.com/

外国人によく聞かれる
日本の宗教
Japanese Religion

James M. Vardaman
ジェームス・M・バーダマン＝著

Sawada Gumi

澤田組＝訳

目 次

はじめに	22

〈日本の宗教入門〉概論　　26

日本人は信仰深いですか？	26
日本人は仏教徒なのですか？	28
なぜ日本人は、神社にも寺にも行くのですか？	30

民間信仰と自然崇拝　　33

日本の自然崇拝とはどのようなものですか？	34
山の神、田の神とは、どのような神様ですか？	34
山岳信仰とは、どのような信仰ですか？	36
富士講とはなんですか？	36
修験道とは、どのような信仰ですか？	38
修験道は仏教？ それとも神道ですか？	38
熊野はなぜ特別な土地なのですか？	40
山伏の装いにはどのような意味があるのですか？	42
怨霊とはなんですか？	46
恐山はなぜ特別な山なのですか？	48
天狗とはなんですか？	50
七福神とはどのような神様ですか？	52

CONTENTS

Foreword	23
Introduction to Japanese Religion	27
Are the Japanese religious?	27
Are the Japanese Buddhists?	29
Why do Japanese go to both shrines and temples?	31
Folk Beliefs and Nature Worship	33
What are the characteristics of Japanese nature worship?	35
What are the *yama-no-kami* and *ta-no-kami*?	35
What is mountain worship?	37
What are the *Fuji-ko*?	37
What kind of religion is *Shugendo*?	39
Is *Shugendo* Buddhist or Shintoist?	39
What is special about the Kumano region?	41
What are the symbolic meanings of the *yamabushi* costume?	43
What is a "vengeful spirit"?	47
What is special about Osorezan?	49
What is a *tengu*?	51
Who are the Seven Deities of Good Fortune?	53

神　道　　57

神道は、どのようにして生まれたのですか？	58
神とは、なんですか？	58
神話にはどのような神様が登場しますか？	60
神に接するときはどうすればよいのですか？	62
八幡とは、どのような神様ですか？	64
稲荷とは、どのような神様ですか？	64
神社とは、どのようなところですか？	66
日本には神社がいくつありますか？	70
神社、神宮、大社の違いはなんですか？	70
礼拝の対象であるご神体は、神社で見ることができますか？	70
祭りとはなんですか？	72
神輿とはなんですか？	72
節分とはなんですか？	74
鳥居とはなんですか？	74
なぜ鳥居は赤く塗られているのですか？	76
手水舎は何をするためにあるのですか？	76
なぜ参道沿いに石灯籠が並んでいるのですか？	78
なぜ神社や寺院の参道には砂利が敷かれているのですか？	78
注連縄とはなんですか？	80
紙垂は何に用いるのですか？	80
拝殿につるしてある鈴は何に使うのですか？	82
神楽とはなんですか？	82
拍手とはなんですか？	82
お賽銭にはどのような意味があるのですか？	84
どうすれば神主（神職）になれるのですか？	86

Shinto   57

How did Shinto develop?	59
What is a *kami*?	59
What *kami* are mentioned in mythology?	61
How should one approach *kami*?	63
What kind of *kami* is Hachiman?	65
What kind of *kami* is Inari?	65
What are the characteristics of a shrine?	67
How many shrines are there in Japan?	71
What is the difference between *jinja*, *jingu* and *taisha*?	71
Can you see the *shintai* (object of worship) inside the shrine?	71
What is a matsuri?	73
What is a mikoshi?	73
What is setsubun?	75
What is a *torii*?	75
Why are *torii* sometimes painted red?	77
What the purpose of the chozuya?	77
Why are there stone lanterns (*ishi-doro*) along the path to a shrine?	79
Why are the *sando* leading to shrines and temples laid with gravel?	79
What is a *shimenawa*?	81
What are *kamishide* used for?	81
What are the bells used for?	83
What is *kagura*?	83
What is *kashiwade*?	83
What is the purpose of *osaisen*?	85
How does one become a Shinto priest (*kannushi*)?	87

項目	ページ
巫女とはなんですか？	88
神道の結婚式とはどのようなものですか？	88
初宮参りとは、なんですか？	90
神職はどのように人々のけがれを清めるのですか？	92
祟りとはなんですか？	92
厄年とはなんですか？ 災いを避けるにはどうすればよいですか？	92
祝詞とはなんですか？	94
神社にはどのように参拝すればよいですか？	94
黄泉の国とはどのようなところですか？	94
神社ではどのような供物(くもつ)を捧げるのですか？	96
けがれとは何ですか？	96
清めの儀式であるお祓いや禊はどのように行われるのですか？	98
夏越の祓とはなんですか？	100
人形(ひとがた)とはなんですか？	100
日本語の"罪"は西洋における"sin"と同義ですか？	100
絵馬とはなんですか？	102
お御籤とはなんですか？ 何が書いてあるのですか？	104
お札とはなんですか？	104
破魔矢とはなんですか？	106
お守りとはなんですか？	106
熊手とはなんですか？	108
へのこ祭、おそそ祭とはどのようなお祭りですか？	108
三種の神器はどこにあるのですか？	108
伊勢神宮 (三重県伊勢市)	110
江戸時代、伊勢神宮への巡礼が突如盛んになったのはなぜですか？	112
出雲大社 (島根県出雲市)	112
明治神宮 (東京都渋谷区)	114
熱田神宮 (愛知県名古屋市)	114

What is a *miko*?	89
What is a Shinto wedding like?	89
What is *hatsu miya mairi*?	91
What does a priest do to purify someone?	93
What is *tatari*?	93
What is *yakudoshi*? How do you avoid danger from it?	93
What are *norito*?	95
How do you worship at a shrine?	95
What is *yomi no kuni* like in Shinto?	95
What kind of offerings do people make at shrines?	97
What is *kegare*?	97
How is "purification" (*oharai* or *misogi*) carried out?	99
What is *Nagoshi-no-harae*?	101
What is *hitogata*?	101
Is *tsumi* the same as the Western idea of "sin"?	101
What is an *ema*?	103
What is an *omikuji* and what does it tell you?	105
What are *ofuda*?	105
What are *hamaya*?	107
What are *omamori*?	107
What are *kumade*?	109
What are the Henoko Matsuri and Ososo Matsuri?	109
Where are the *sanshu no jingi*, the three imperial regalia?	109
Ise Shrine (Mie prefecture)	111
Why were there sudden pilgrimages to the Grand Ise Shrine during the Edo period?	113
Izumo Taisha Shrine (Shimane prefecture)	113
Meiji Shrine (Tokyo)	115
Atsuta Shrine (Nagoya)	115

湯島天神（東京都文京区）	116
鶴岡八幡宮（神奈川県鎌倉市）	116
日光東照宮（栃木県日光市）	116
平安神宮（京都府京都市）	118
伏見稲荷大社（京都府京都市）	118
葵祭とはどのような祭りですか？	120
祇園祭とはどのような祭りですか？	120
厳島神社（広島県廿日市市）	120
地鎮祭や鍬入れは何のために行うのですか？	122
建築中の家屋についている豪華な飾りはなんですか？	124
神棚とはなんですか？	124
門松とはなんですか？	126
鏡餅とはなんですか？	126
初詣でとはなんですか？	126
相撲と神道は関係があるのですか？	128
国家神道とはなんですか？	130
靖国神社の何が問題なのですか？	130

神道と仏教のつながり　　135

神社と寺院が同じ場所に建っていることがあるのは 　なぜですか？	136
なぜ神道と仏教は切り離されたのですか？	136
なぜ明治時代に反仏教運動が起きたのですか？	138
現代の日本人は、仏教もしくは神道を信仰しているのですか？	138

Yushima Tenjin (Tokyo)	117
Tsurugaoka Hachiman-gu (Kamakura)	117
Toshogu (Nikko in Tochigi prefecture)	117
Heian Shrine (Kyoto)	119
Fushimi Inari Taisha (Kyoto)	119
What is the Aoi Festival?	121
What is the Gion Festival?	121
Itsukushima Jinja (Hiroshima prefecture)	121
Why do people perform *jichinsai* and *kuwaire*?	123
What are those elaborate decorations on the houses under construction?	125
What is a *kamidana*?	125
What is a *kadomatsu*?	127
What is *kagami-mochi*?	127
What is *hatsumode*?	127
Is *sumo* part of Shinto?	129
What was "State Shinto," *Kokka Shinto*?	131
Why is there controversy about Yasukuni Shrine?	131

Connections between Shinto and Buddhism 135

Why are a shrine and a temple sometimes found in the same place?	137
Why were Shinto and Buddhism completely separated?	137
Why was there an anti-Buddhist movement during the Meiji period?	139
Are Japanese today believers in Buddhism or Shintoism?	139

仏　教　143

仏教とはどういうものですか？　144
仏教が大きく分裂した際の流派にはどんなものがありますか？　146
仏教はどのようにして日本にやって来たのですか？　148
奈良時代と平安時代、仏教はどのように受け入れられていたのですか？　148
奈良時代と平安時代の間に仏教はどのように変わったのですか？　150
仏教は初め、どのようにして死や葬式と結びつくようになったのですか？　152
仏教における「来世(らいせ)」とはどのようなものですか？　154
「末法」とはどんなものですか？　154
経典(「お経」)とはどんなものですか？　156
人はなぜ、お経を毛筆で書き写すのですか？　158
仏像を彫ることはどんな功徳(くどく)がありますか？　158
禅とは、どんなものですか？　158
空海とはどんな人物でしたか？　160
真言宗とは、どんなものですか？　162
最澄とはどんな人物でしたか？　162
天台宗とは、どんなものですか？　164
法然とは、どんな人物でしたか？　166
浄土宗とは、どんなものですか？　168
親鸞とは、どんな人物でしたか？　168
浄土真宗とは、どんなものですか？　170
日蓮とは、どんな人物でしたか？　170
日蓮宗とは、どんなものですか？　172
一遍とは、どんな人物でしたか？　172
栄西とは、どんな人物でしたか？　174
道元とは、どんな人物でしたか？　176

Buddhism 143

What is Buddhism?	145
What are the main types of Buddhism?	147
How did Buddhism come to Japan?	149
How was Buddhism received in Nara and Heian periods?	149
How did Buddhism change between the Nara and Heian periods?	151
How did Buddhism first become associated with death and funerals?	153
What is "the afterlife" like in Buddhism?	155
What is *mappo*?	155
What are sutras (*okyo*)?	157
Why do people copy sutras with brush and ink?	159
What is gained by carving a Buddhist image?	159
What is Zen?	159
Who was Kukai?	161
What is the Shingon sect?	163
Who was Saicho?	163
What is the Tendai sect?	165
Who was Honen?	167
What is the Jodo Sect?	169
Who was Shinran?	169
What is the Jodo Shin Sect?	171
Who was Nichiren?	171
What is the Nichiren Sect?	173
Who was Ippen?	173
Who was Eisai?	175
Who was Dogen?	177

鈴木大拙とは、どんな人物でしたか？	178
仏尊には、主にどんな種類のものがありますか？	178
像の仏が踏みつけている奇妙な生き物は何ものですか？	184
仏陀はなぜ巻き毛で大きな耳をしているのですか？	184
仏像の眉間には、なぜほくろのようなものがあるのですか？	186
不動明王とは、どういうものですか？	186
なぜ地蔵は、それほど人に好まれるのですか？	188
なぜ観音は、それほど人に好まれるのですか？	188
「阿修羅」とはどんなものですか？	190
「だるま」とは、どんなものですか？	190
「大仏」については、どんなことが知られていますか？	192
お寺とは、どんな造りになっていますか？	192
仏塔とは、どんなものですか？	196
日本に、お寺はいくつあるのですか？	196
なぜお寺の正面には一対の狛犬がいるのですか？	196
お寺の門のところに立っている、恐ろしい二人組の「仁王」とはどんなものですか？	198
「地獄絵図」が意図するものとは何ですか？	198
なぜ仏像には卍(「万字」)の印があるのですか？	200
現在、日本仏教の主な僧院はどこにあるのですか？	200
「駆け込み寺」とはどんなものですか？	202
なぜ僧は剃髪するのですか？	204
「袈裟」が象徴するものとはなんですか？	204
なぜ僧は数珠を持っているのですか？	204
日本の仏僧は結婚できるのですか？	206
なぜそれほど多くのお寺が、家業のようにして運営されているのですか？	206
お寺はどのようにして収入を得ているのですか？	206

Who was Daisetsu Suzuki?	179
What are the main kinds of Buddhist deities?	179
Who are the strange creatures that statues of Buddha step on?	185
Why does the Buddha have curly hair and big ears?	185
Why do Buddhist statues have a mole in the middle of the brow?	187
What is Fudo Myoo?	187
Why is Jizo so popular?	189
Why is Kannon so popular?	189
What is an *asura*?	191
What is a *daruma*?	191
What makes a statue a *daibutsu*?	193
What defines a temple?	193
What is a pagoda?	197
How many temples are there in Japan?	197
Why is there a pair of lions in front of a temple?	197
What are the pair of fierce *Nio* in temple gates?	199
What is the purpose of a "hell screen" (*jigoku-ezu*)?	199
Why is there a swastika (*manji*) in Buddhist images?	201
Where are the main Buddhist monasteries today?	201
What are "refuge temples" (*kakekomidera*)?	203
Why do priests shave their heads?	205
What is the symbolism of a surplice (*kesa*)?	205
Why do priests carry prayer beads?	205
Can Japanese Buddhist priests marry?	207
Why are so many temples run like a family business?	207
How does a temple receive income?	207

項目	頁
「檀家」の役割とはどんなものですか？	208
仏教美術に出てくる象徴的な生き物には、どんなものがありますか？	210
「千社札」とは、どんなものですか？	212
お寺では、どのようにして参拝するのですか？	212
「護摩」とはどんなものですか？	212
「南無阿弥陀仏」とは、どんな意味ですか？	214
「妙法蓮華経」とは、どんな意味ですか？	214
浅草寺（浅草観音）の始まりとは、どんなものですか？	214
浅草寺の門はなぜ「雷門」と呼ばれるのですか？	216
参拝客は、なぜ浅草寺で線香を上げるのですか？	218
成田山（新勝寺）	218
鎌倉大仏	218
清水寺	220
銀閣寺（慈照寺）	220
金閣寺（鹿苑寺）	222
三十三間堂（蓮華王院）	222
東大寺	224
「お水取り」とはどんなものですか？	226
法隆寺（奈良近郊）	226
なぜ仏教徒は火葬し、遺骨をお墓に入れるのですか？	228
死後、「法事」は何回行われるのですか？	228
「仏壇」とは、どんなものですか？	230
「位牌」とは、どんなものですか？	230
なぜ死者には戒名が与えられるのですか？	232
「卒塔婆」とは、どんなものですか？	232
「お盆」とはどんな日なのですか？	232
曼荼羅とは、どんなものですか？	234
京都の「五山送り火」とはどんなものですか？	236

What is the role of *danka*?	209
What animal symbols appear in Buddhism iconography?	211
What are *senja fuda*?	213
How does one worship at a temple?	213
What is a *goma* ceremony?	213
What is the meaning of "*Namu Amida Butsu*"?	215
What is the meaning of "*Myoho Renge-kyo*"?	215
What is the origin of Senso-ji (Asakusa Kannon)?	215
Why is the gate called "*Kaminari-mon*"?	217
Why do visitors burn incense at Sensoji?	219
Narita-san (Shinshoji)	219
Kamakura Daibutsu	219
Kiyomizu-dera	221
Ginkaku-ji (Jisho-ji)	221
Kinkaku-ji (Rokuon-ji)	223
Sanjusangendo (Rengeoin)	223
Todai-ji	225
What is *Omizutori*?	227
Horyuji (near Nara)	227
Why do Buddhists cremate and put the remains in a grave?	229
How many memorial services, *hoji*, are held after death?	229
What is a *butsudan*?	231
What is a memorial tablet?	231
Why are the dead given Buddhist names?	233
What is a *sotoba*?	233
What happens at *O-bon*?	233
What is a mandala?	235
What is the *okuribi* of the Gozan in Kyoto?	237

「彼岸」とはどんなものですか？	238
「墓参り」とは、どんなものですか？	238
「花祭」とは、どんなものですか？	238
「千日回峰行」とはどんなものですか？	240
「即身成仏」とはどんなものですか？	242
人はなぜ四国八十八箇所巡礼(じゅんれい)をするのですか？	242
他には、どんな巡礼があるのですか？	246
「あみだくじ」は、なぜそう呼ばれるのですか？	246
なぜ大晦日の夜に鐘を108回鳴らすのですか？	248

日本のキリスト教　251

誰が、いつキリスト教を日本にもたらしたのですか？	252
誰が、なぜキリスト教を受け入れたのですか？	252
キリスト教は、なぜ禁じられたのですか？	254
「隠れキリシタン」とは、どんなものですか？	254
キリスト教の禁止は、いつ解かれたのですか？	256
キリスト教が日本に与えた影響とは、どんなものですか？	256
キリスト教式の結婚式を挙げる日本人がいるのはなぜですか？	258

新興宗教と新新興宗教　261

いわゆる「新興宗教」とはどんなものですか？	262
天理教とは、どんなものですか？	264
金光教とは、どんなものですか？	264
大本教とは、どんなものですか？	266
PL教団とは、どんなものですか？	266
生長の家とは、どんなものですか？	268

What is *higan*?	239
What is *haka mairi*?	239
What is *hana matsuri*?	239
What is *sennichi kaihogyo*?	241
What is *sokushin jobutsu*?	243
Why do people undertake the Shikoku 88-temple pilgrimage?	243
What other pilgrimages are there?	247
Why is one form of drawing lots called *Amida-kuji*?	247
Why do people ring temple bells 108 times on New Year's Eve?	249

Christianity in Japan   251

Who brought Christianity to Japan and when?	253
Who accepted Christianity and why?	253
Why was Christianity banned?	255
What are "hidden Christians" (*kakure kirishitan*)?	255
When was Christianity permitted again?	257
What impact has Christianity had on Japan?	257
Why do some Japanese have Christian weddings?	259

New Religions and New-New Religions 261

What are the so-called "New Religions"?	263
What is Tenrikyo?	265
What is Konko-kyo?	265
What is Omoto-kyo?	267
What is PL Kyodan?	267
What is Seicho no Ie?	269

霊友会とは、どんなものですか？	268
創価学会とは、どんなものですか？	270
立正佼成会とは、どんなものですか？	272
阿含宗とは、どんなものですか？	274
オウム真理教（アーレフ）とは、どんなものですか？	274
白光真宏会とは、どんなものですか？	276

宗教的意味合いを含む儀式と社会の風習　279

年中行事	280
日本人が忌み嫌うものとは、どんなものですか？	288
仏教で禁じられている食べ物には、どんなものがありますか？	290
「六曜」とはどんなものですか？	290
「十二支」とはどんなものですか？	292
「流鏑馬」とはどんなものですか？	294
「パワースポット」とは、どんなものですか？	296
付録：日本の仏教宗派	298

What is Reiyukai?	269
What is Soka Gakkai?	271
What is Rissho Koseikai?	273
What is Agon-shu?	275
What is Aum Shinrikyo (Aleph)?	275
What is Byakko Shinkokai?	277

Ceremonies and social customs (semi-religious, cross-religion) 279

Annual events	281
What taboos do Japanese follow?	289
What foods were taboo according to Buddhism?	291
What are the *rokuyo*?	291
What are the animals of the Chinese zodiac (*junishi*)?	293
What is *yabusame*?	295
What are "power spots"?	297
Appendix: The Buddhist Sect of Japan	299
Bibliography	300

はじめに

　日本を訪れる外国人にとって、この国の宗教文化はたいへん興味深いものです。彼らの興味は神社仏閣にとどまらず、儀式、習慣、歴史、建築など多岐に及びます。ところが、特定の宗教を信仰し、それについて詳しく語れる人々を除けば、日本人の多様な信仰を外国人に説明できる日本人はほとんどいません。

　本書は、外国人観光客が日本の宗教文化について抱きそうな疑問をまとめたものです。多くの場合、詳しすぎる説明は歓迎されないでしょう。日本の習慣や日本人の考え方が理解できるような、シンプルかつ明解な答えが求められます。さらに、日本人にとっては当たり前に思われることや、説明の仕様がないことに関する質問を受けることも少なくないことでしょう。本書では、こうした質問にも特別な注意を払いました。

　外国からの観光客は目に映るものすべてに好奇心を抱き、それが何なのか、どういう意味かを知りたいと思っています。そこで本書は、神社仏閣だけでなく、たとえば「鳥居」など、宗教関連のものについても取り上げました。外国人に人気の観光スポットや、その地において特筆すべきものにとくに力を入れています。また、日本人からすれば

Foreword

Foreign visitors to Japan are interested in all aspects of its culture, including religious sites, ceremonies, customs, history and architecture. With the exception of devout believers in a particular religion who can tell you in detail about what their religion believes, most Japanese seem to find it difficult to explain various aspects of Japanese religion to foreign visitors.

This volume covers the kinds of questions that foreign visitors are most likely to ask. Visitors are usually not interested in long explanations filled with dates and details. They prefer a simple, clear explanation that helps them to understand the customs of Japan and the way Japanese think. Furthermore, foreign visitors often ask questions about things that Japanese take for granted and find hard to explain. Special attention is paid to these kinds of questions.

Sightseers from abroad are curious about what they see and would like to know what it is and what meaning it has. Therefore, we include both physical objects, such as a *torii*, and certain sightseeing destinations that have religious connections. The focus is on some popular destinations among visitors and on special

宗教とは無関係と思われるものも登場します。言い換えれば、この本は日本人の「宗教」と「宗教的態度」について、宗派・宗教を超えた広い視野で説明しています。

　やむを得ず難解な専門用語を使用する場合もありますが、本書の目的はあくまでも「基本の説明」という実用性にあります。そこで、説明文は可能な限り簡潔なものとし、みなさんが自信をもって活用できるよう、できるだけシンプルな英文を心がけました。

　英語と日本語の対訳式のメリットとして、辞書を引く手間が省けることをあげておきます。難解な用語は、参照しやすいように太字で示しました。

　日本の宗教はときに曖昧で、「民間信仰」「神道」「仏教」のどのカテゴリーに属するのか判断が難しいものもありました。たとえば「七福神」は、この3つのカテゴリーすべてに当てはまるものです。それゆえ、複数のセクションにわたって登場する項目もあります。

features of those sites. We will also look at subjects that to Japanese may not seem particularly religious or connected to a religion. In other words, this volume considers "religion" and "religious behavior" in a broad sense, not in a narrow, sectarian sense.

While it is not possible to avoid difficult terminology, this volume aims for practical application by explaining just the basics. Therefore, the explanations are kept as short as possible. Further, explanations are given in English that is as simple as possible, so that you can use them with confidence.

The advantage of an English-Japanese *taiyaku* format is that the reader will not need to constantly refer to a dictionary. Where a term is particularly difficult, it will be put in bold type in both the English and Japanese for quick reference. Some background explanations will be given only in Japanese, for simple reference.

Because Japanese religion is sometimes ambiguous, it is not always easy to categorize elements under Folk Beliefs, Shinto, or Buddhism. For example, the Seven Deities of Good Fortune could fit in all of these three categories. Therefore, where it is necessary, key subjects will appear in multiple sections.

〈日本の宗教入門〉概論

 以下にあげる質疑応答は、本文で取り上げるには難しいテーマです。他の項目に比べ、文章にすると難しくなってしまいます。しかしこれは、日本を訪れる観光客の多くが抱く疑問です。まずは、ここからスタートしましょう。

■日本人は信仰深いですか?

 日本人は、自分は信仰深い人間ではないと考える傾向があります。ほとんどの日本人は、意図的になんらかの宗教団体に「加入」することがないからです。また多くの人が、仏教の教義や神道の詳細について、あまり関心を払っていないことも理由として挙げられます。

 しかし、新年の初めに神社や寺を訪れる「初詣で」や、家族の墓を訪れる「お墓参り」といった"宗教的"なイベントを日本人が実践しているのも事実です。彼らは健康や合格、ビジネスでの成功を祈ったりもします。

 西洋的な感覚においては、日本人は信仰深くないといってかまわないでしょう。しかし文化的な意味において、彼らは信仰に厚いのです。そこが、日本のユニークな点といえるでしょう。

Introduction to Japanese Religion

The following questions and answers are a bit more difficult than those in the main part of this book. Therefore, the language is somewhat more challenging. But these are questions that most foreign visitors to Japan will wonder about, so we will consider them here at the very start.

◼ Are the Japanese religious?

Japanese tend to say that they are not religious. This is partly because the majority does not make a conscious decision to "join" a religious group. And it is partly because most do not pay much attention to the doctrines of the sects of Buddhism or the details of the *kami* of the Shinto shrines they visit.

However, they do participate in "religious" events such as *hatsumode* (the first visit of the year to a shrine or temple) and *ohaka mairi* (visiting the family tomb). They do pray for good health, success on examinations and prosperity in business.

It is safe to say that they are not religious in the Western sense. But they are religious in a cultural sense that is somewhat unique to Japan.

◼日本人は仏教徒なのですか?

　江戸時代（1603-1868）、幕府の命令ですべての家庭、国民が「仏教徒」になりました。当時の幕府はキリスト教を危険とみなし、弾圧していました。幕府は国民にキリスト教徒ではない証しとして、仏教寺院に檀家登録するよう求めたのです。

　正式な登録をしないと、結婚の登録や、旅行の際に必要な通行証を手に入れることもできませんでした。さらには、キリスト教の信者であると疑われることにもなりました。そこで各家庭ごとに近くの寺院や少し離れた人気の寺院、あるいは人気の僧侶がいる寺院に赴き、家族全員の登録を行いました。各寺院はそれぞれの檀家からのみ、葬儀や法要の際のお布施という形で援助を受けました。仏教が主として死と関係の深い宗教であるという考えは、このとき生まれました。

　このシステムはまた、僧侶を公僕にかえました。彼らの仕事は、説法を説き、人々を悟りへ導き、困っている民衆を助けることではなく、地域住民の登録を行い、幕府に代わって記録をつけることになったからです。その結果、仏教は活気を失い、多くの人々が僧侶や寺院に憤りを感じるようになりました。とはいえ、地域の僧侶は檀家にとって大切な「葬儀」を執り行なっていたのです。

　現代の日本人は、自分の家がどの宗派の寺に属するのか、たぶん知りません。彼らにとって大した問題ではないので

▣ Are the Japanese Buddhists?

During the Tokugawa period (1603–1868), every member of every family became "Buddhist." They were required to do this by the Bakufu, the military government. The Bakufu felt Christianity was a dangerous religion and suppressed it. The Bakufu required Japanese to prove that they were *not* Christian, by having them register as a parishioner of a Buddhist temple.

Without a formal registration, people could not register marriages or get official passes for travel outside the local area. They would also be suspected of believing in Christianity. So, each family naturally went to the closest temple, a popular temple not too far away, or a temple with a popular priest and registered every member of the family as a parishioner. The temples received support only from their members. It came in the form of donations, made on occasions such as funerals and memorial services. This created the idea that Buddhism is primarily a religion related to death.

This system also turned the Buddhist priests into civil servants. Their job was not to preach Buddhism, lead people to enlightenment, or help them in times of trouble. Their job was to register local residents and keep track of them for the government. As a result, Buddhism lost its vitality and many people came to resent the priests and temples. However, the local temple priest did perform a valuable service for members: holding funeral rites.

す。各宗派の教義の違いもおそらく知らないでしょう。仏教を身近に学ぶ機会はほとんどありません。自らの死が近づいたり、親しい家族が亡くなるまでは。

◪ なぜ日本人は、神社にも寺にも行くのですか？

基本的に、宗教に関して言えば、日本人は排他的ではありません。神も仏もその他の精霊も、わたしたち人間にご利益をもたらしてくれる存在です。ですから日本人の多くは、神社で健康を祈願し、新年に寺にお参りし、キリスト教式の結婚式を挙げることも平気です。日本人にとって、それはまったく矛盾してはいないのです。

しかし、こうしたことがふつうに行われていることを理解するのは大切です。さまざまな"宗教的"行事に参加するために、特定の信仰や宗派に対する義務や献身は求められません。ただ単に助けやご利益や保護を求め、感謝の気持ちを表すために祈り、儀式を行い、祝詞やお経を唱え、神社仏閣を訪れます。歴史を通じて、日本人はそうしてきました。そして今も、その伝統を守り続けています。

Japanese today may not know which sect their "family temple" belongs to. It does not really matter to them. They may not know the particular teachings of that sect or other sects. And they have few occasions or little motivation to learn about Buddhism—until they get closer to the end or their life or until a close family member dies.

◼ Why do Japanese go to both shrines and temples?

Basically Japanese are not exclusive when it comes to religion. *Kami*, Buddhas and other spirits have *riyaku*—powers and benefits that can be passed on to human beings. So, most Japanese do not hesitate to pray to Shinto *kami* for health, visit Buddhist temples at New Years and be married in a Christian-style wedding ceremony. They see no conflict in this at all.

However, it is important to realize that participation in such actions is rather casual. Participating in these various "religious" events does not require a commitment to a particular belief or to a particular sect of a religion. You simply ask for help, benefit or protection or express gratitude by means of prayer, ritual, chanting or visiting a place of worship. Throughout history, Japanese have done this. They are simply maintaining that tradition.

Folk Beliefs and Nature Worship

民間信仰と自然崇拝

■日本の自然崇拝とはどのようなものですか?

古代の日本人は、自然のいたるところに神が宿り、森羅万象をつかさどっていると信じていました。人々は自然と自然の持つ力を畏れ、敬いました。川や滝、海では心身を洗い清める「祓い」が行われ、山はとりわけ重要な崇拝対象となりました。

自然が**神聖視**されたのは、神が創ったものだからという理由だけではありませんでした。古代日本人は、美しい自然そのものが神聖だと考えていたのです。そのため、自然の力を秘めた美しい場所に神社が建てられました。

古代人のように熱心な信仰ではないものの、**自然崇拝**は今も日本人の**信仰心**の根底に息づいています。

■山の神、田の神とは、どのような神様ですか?

古代の日本では、山の頂きには**神**が住んでいると考えられていました。山の神は、種まきをする春から**収穫**の秋のあいだ、田畑に下りてきて田の神になります。農村では、春に田の神を迎える祭りを行い、収穫の季節になると、山へ帰る神に感謝の気持ちを表しました。

◙ What are the characteristics of Japanese nature worship?

Ancient Japanese believed nature was the place where *kami* lived and interacted between heaven and earth. They had a deep appreciation and respect for nature and its powers. They used rivers, waterfalls and the ocean to perform **purification** (*harai*). Mountain worship became especially important.

These ancient people believed nature was **sacred** not just because it was created by the *kami*. They believed that places of beauty were sacred by themselves. Therefore, they created shrines at sites of natural power and beauty.

Today **nature worship** underlies Japanese **religiosity**, even though it is not as obvious as it was in ancient times.

◙ What are the *yama-no-kami* and *ta-no-kami*?

In ancient Japan, people believed that **deities** (*kami*) lived on the tops of mountains. During the rice-growing season, the *yama-no-kami* (mountain deities) came down to the fields from the spring planting to the autumn **harvest**. Farmers greeted them as the local *ta-no-kami*, deities of the fields, with a festival in the spring. At harvest time, the farmers expressed their gratitude to the deities, which then returned to the mountains.

◼山岳信仰とは、どのような信仰ですか？

　山が長いあいだ崇拝されてきた理由は三つあります。まず、山そのものが神とみなされていたためです。二つめは、山には子孫を見守る死者の霊や、春に山から下りてきて収穫が終わると帰っていく田の神など、さまざまな神が住んでいると考えられていたためです。三つめは、山は死者の住む「他界」に近いと考えられていたためです。山の頂きでは、死者の霊とより交信しやすいとされました。

　御嶽山（長野・岐阜県境）や恐山（青森県）、富士山は特に多くの崇拝を集めました。富士山は古代より山の女神として崇められ、平安時代には山岳信仰のひとつである修験道の中心地になりました。富士登山には古くから宗教的な意味合いがあり、清めのための行為としても考えられています。

恐山（青森県）

◼富士講とはなんですか？

　江戸時代、富士山頂を目指す巡礼が盛んになりました。しかし、山までの旅や登山にはお金がかかります。そこで多くの人々が富士講と呼ばれる団体に加わりました。富士講では、講員たちからお金を集め、毎年くじ引きで数名の登山者を選びます。富士登山に行けない人々も富士を拝めるようにするため、富士山から持ち帰った

◉ What is mountain worship?

Mountains were long worshipped for three reasons. First, they were considered to be *kami* (deities). Second, they were considered to be places where deities live. These deities included the spirits of the dead who assisted the living. They also included *ta-no-kami*, the *kami* of the rice fields, who descended to the fields in the spring and return to the mountains after the harvest. Third, they were closer to the "other world." It is easier to communicate with the **spirits** of the dead from the top of a mountain.

Mountains such as Mt. Ontake (on the border of Nagano and Gifu prefectures), Mt. Osore (Aomori prefecture) and Mt. Fuji were considered especially auspicious. In ancient times, people worshipped Mt. Fuji as a female mountain deity. In the Heian period, Mt. Fuji became a center of *Shugendo*, a kind of mountain worship. Climbing Mt. Fuji has been a religious act for centuries, and it is often seen as an act of purification.

◉ What are the *Fuji-ko*?

Making a pilgrimage to the top of Mt. Fuji became popular during the Edo period. But traveling to the mountain and climbing it cost money. Many people joined associations called *Fuji-ko*, which collected money from members. Each year one or more members were chosen by **lottery** to climb Mt. Fuji. Not everyone could climb the mountain, so members built miniatures

岩などを積みあげた小山が江戸中に造られました。

■修験道とは、どのような信仰ですか？

修験道は、山岳信仰やアニミズム、原始神道、仏教の**密教思想**が融合してできた日本古来の宗教的な修行法です。7世紀の呪術者である役行者（えんのぎょうじゃ）という人物が始めたとされます。

修験道の**修行者**を山伏（やまぶし）といいます。山伏は山中に入り込み、**難行**（なんぎょう）・**苦行**（くぎょう）を重ねます。肉体と自然が触れあうことにより、霊的な能力を高められると考えられています。

■修験道は仏教？ それとも神道ですか？

修験道は山岳信仰と密教が融合した宗教です。平安時代、仏教徒たちが独りで山にこもり、修行をしたり**経典**を唱えたりするようになったのが始まりとされています。12世紀までには、ひとつの宗教として確立しました。

修験道を実践する人々を山伏といい、文字通り、「山に伏す者」という意味があります。天台宗と真言宗の二つの宗派に分かれています。山伏は季節ごとに神聖な山に登る「峰入り」（みねいり）といわれる修行を行います。大峰山（おおみねさん）や出羽三山（でわさんざん）（羽黒山・月山・湯殿山）、熊野周辺の山などをはじめとする山々で霊力を身につけ、悟りを得て仏

湯殿山神社大鳥居（山形県）

of the mountain around the city of Edo, using rocks brought down from the mountain.

🔲 What kind of religion is *Shugendo*?

Shugendo is an ancient religious practice that combines mountain worship, **folk animism**, ancient Shinto beliefs and **esoteric Buddhism**. The mystic En no Gyoja is considered to have organized *Shugendo* in the 7th century.

Yamabushi, **practitioners** of *Shugendo*, carry out **rigorous rituals and challenging treks** through the mountains. They believe that by coming into physical contact with nature they can increase their spiritual experience and power.

🔲 Is *Shugendo* Buddhist or Shintoist?

Shugendo is a religious order that combines worship of mountains with esoteric Buddhism. *Shugendo* began in the Heian period with the solitary Buddhist hermits who carried out ascetic practices on certain mountains and recited certain **Buddhist scriptures**. By the 12th century, it was a distinct religion.

Those who practice *Shugendo* are known as *yamabushi*, literally "one who lies in the mountains." These men are affiliated with either Tendai or Shingon Buddhism. They perform ritual exercises called "entering the mountains" (*mineiri*), going up sacred mountains considered sacred, during each of the four seasons. On mountains such as Ominesan, the Dewa

になることを目指すのです。

山伏には**魔除け**や癒しの力があるとされています。焚き火から取り出した**熾火**の上を歩く「火渡り」という**儀式**も有名です。火渡りをすることで、山中の修行で身につけた力を示します。山伏はまた、不動明王など炎を操る神仏に庶民の除災招福を祈願します。

1868年の**明治維新**前まで、修験道の修行や儀式は土着の宗教や仏教、神道など多様な要素が混じり合ったものでした。しかし維新後、新政府による**神仏分離**政策の一環として、仏教系の宗教団体としての活動を強いられました。

■熊野はなぜ特別な土地なのですか？

日本に仏教が伝来した6世紀、熊野は神道の自然崇拝と密教の**苦行**とが融合した修行の地となりました。熊野にある三つの神社を表す熊野三山は、仏教徒にとっての楽園である**浄土**の象徴とみなされるようになりました。三山のひとつ、熊野那智大社では那智の滝を祀っています。熊野三山は、重要な**巡礼地**のひとつとなっており、いくつかの巡礼ルートがあります。京都から熊野三山を巡るルートは、およそ800キロメー

Sanzan (Haguro-san, Gassan and Yudono-san), and the mountains around Kumano, *yamabushi* try to gain magic powers and transform themselves into a Buddha.

The *yamabushi* perform **exorcisms** and healing. They are also known for "fire-walking" (*hiwatari*), which means walking across the **embers** of a ritual bonfire. The ritual illustrates the powers they have harnessed through their practices in the mountains. They call on the powers of deities associated with fire, such as Fudo, to bring beneficial and purifying powers to ordinary people.

Until the **Meiji Restoration** (1868), the *yamabushi* had been highly eclectic in employing rites and practices from native religions, Buddhism and Shinto. But after the Restoration, they were forced to register as practitioners of Buddhist sects, as part of the government **separation of Shinto and Buddhism**.

◼ What is special about the Kumano region?

Buddhism was introduced to Japan in the 6th century. In the Kumano region, the Shinto worship of nature absorbed the **ascetic practices** of esoteric Buddhism. The Kumano Sanzan, "three shrines of Kumano," came to be seen as representing the **Pure Land**, the Buddhist paradise. One of them, the Kumano Nachi Taisha, is dedicated to the worship of the Nachi waterfalls. The shrines became an important **destination for pilgrimages**. One route from Kyoto was close to 800

トルあります。もうひとつ、高野山から熊野を巡るルートはより険しい道のりで、1000メートル超の山を三つ越えなければなりません。

◨山伏の装いにはどのような意味があるのですか?

山伏が身につける十六道具には、それぞれ実用的な用途と象徴的な意味があります。

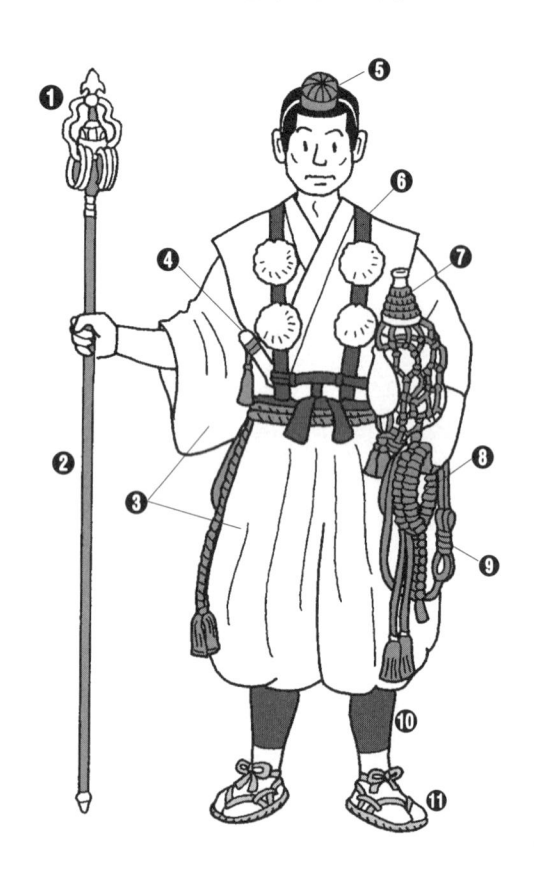

kilometers (500 miles). Another more difficult route connected Mt. Koya with Kumano and crossed three mountain passes rising over 1,000 meters (3,300 feet).

◼ What are the symbolic meanings of the *yamabushi* costume?

There are 16 items in the traditional costume of the *yamabushi* that have both practical use and symbolic meaning.

①錫杖	Shakujo
②金剛杖	Kongozue
③鈴懸	Suzukake
④柴打	Shiba-uchi
⑤頭巾	Tokin
⑥結袈裟	Yuigesa
⑦法螺	Hora
⑧苛高数珠	Irataka no juzu
⑨走縄	Hashiri nawa
⑩脚半	Kyahan
⑪草鞋	Waraji

Folk Beliefs and Nature Worship

（1）頭巾は、黒い小さな帽子で、大日如来（梵名をマハー・ヴァイローチャナといいます）の宝冠を象徴しています。
（2）綾藺笠は、藺草で編んだ笠で、修験者を育てる**母胎**を象徴しています。
（3）鈴懸は、修験者の正装で、上下に分かれています。上着は金剛界曼荼羅を、袴は胎蔵界曼荼羅を象徴しています。
（4）結袈裟は、六つの飾り房がついた帯状の布です。金剛界曼荼羅と胎蔵界曼荼羅を象徴しています。
（5）法螺は、合図を送ったり、経を唱える拍子をとったりするために吹く**ホラガイ**です。大日如来の教えを象徴しています。
（6）苛高数珠は、108個の小さな珠が連ねられ、**世俗**から神聖なものへの移り変わりを象徴しています。
（7）錫杖は、僧侶などが持つ杖で、**成仏**の象徴です。
（8）笈は、崇拝する物や経典、修行に必要なものを入れて運ぶ箱です。
（9）片箱は、笈の上に重ねて背負う箱です。金剛界曼荼羅と胎蔵界曼荼羅の**結合**を象徴しています。
（10）金剛杖は、山を登るときに突く白木の**杖**です。煩悩をくだき悟りをひらく成仏を象徴しています。
（11）引敷は、座って休むときに使う敷物で、**罪**の浄化を象徴しています。
（12）脚半は、山を登るときに脚を保護するために

(1) *Tokin*, a small black skullcap, symbolizes Mahavairocana (known in Japanese as Dainichi)
(2) *Ayaigasa*, a straw hat, symbolizes the growth of the practitioner in the **womb**
(3) *Suzukake*, the **formal robe** of the practitioner, consists of two parts: the upper garment symbolizes the Diamond Mandala, and the lower garment (*hakama*) symbolizes the Womb Mandala
(4) *Yuigesa*, a surplice, has six colored tassels and symbolizes the womb-and-diamond mandala
(5) *Hora*, a **conch shell**, signals and sets the rhythm for sutra readings and symbolizes the preaching of Mahavairocana
(6) *Irataka no juzu*, a 108-bead rosary, symbolizes the transformation from **secular** to sacred
(7) *Shakujo*, a priest's staff, is a walking stick and symbolizes **becoming a Buddha**
(8) *Oi*, a wooden box, carries objects of worship, scriptures and ritual tools
(9) *Katabako*, a shoulder box, placed over the *oi* symbolizes **communion** of the diamond and womb mandala
(10) *Kongozue*, a **cane**, is used for climbing and symbolizes becoming a Buddha
(11) *Hitsushiki*, a sitting mat, is used for resting and symbolizes purification of **sin**
(12) *Kyahan*, leggings, protect the legs during climbs and symbolize becoming a Buddha

まとう布で、成仏を象徴しています。
(13) 桧扇(ひせん)は、儀式において焚火を**あおぐ**のに使います。不動明王が邪悪を滅ぼすさまを象徴しています。
(14) 柴打(しばうち)は、火を燃やす**儀式**に使う木を切るための刀で、不動明王を象徴しています。
(15) 走縄は、修行に使われる道具で、不動明王を象徴しています。
(16) 草鞋(わらじ)は、わらの履物で、仏が乗っている**蓮**の花を象徴しています。

■ 怨霊とはなんですか?

怨霊または御霊とは、殺されたり、恨みをもったまま死んだりした身分の高い人々の邪悪な霊です。怨霊の**呪い**は、地震や雷、台風などの自然**災害**となって降りかかってくると考えられました。こうした怨霊として、平安時代の二人の人物がとりわけよく知られています。

菅原道真（845-903）は、対立していた藤原氏の策略により天皇への謀反の疑いをかけられ、九州の大宰府へ**左遷**されてしまいました。その地で**潔白**を訴える歌をいくつも書き残したあと、道真は生涯を閉じました。ところが道真の死後、京都の宮中(きゅうちゅう)では不幸がたてつづけに起こります。火事や洪水が起こり、何人もの死者が出ました。人々は、これは道真の怨霊の仕業(しわざ)で、自分を**陥れた**人間に**復讐**しようとしているのだと考えました。

(13) *Hisen*, a cypress fan, is used for **fanning** a sacred fire and symbolizes Fudo Myoo's actions in destroying evil

(14) *Shiba-uchi*, wood-cutter, is used for cutting wood for the fire **rite** and symbolizes Fudo Myoo

(15) *Hashiri nawa*, a rope, is used in ascetic practices and symbolizes Fudo Myoo's activities

(16) *Waraji*, straw sandals, serve as footwear and symbolize the **lotus**, seat of the Buddha

▣ What is a "vengeful spirit"?

"**Vengeful spirits**," *onryo* or *goryo*, are the evil spirits of people of high rank who were either killed or died in anger. The **curse** of vengeful spirits was held to take the form of natural **calamities**, such as earthquakes, lightning and typhoons. Among the most famous of these supposed spirits are two from the Heian period.

Sugawara no Michizane (845–903) opposed the power of the Fujiwara family. He was falsely accused of plotting against the imperial court. As a result, he **was sent into exile** at Dazaifu in Kyushu. He died there after writing a series of famous poems protesting his **innocence**. After his death, a number of misfortunes occurred at the court in Kyoto, including fire, flood, and unexpected deaths. Some people believed these misfortunes were caused by his angry spirit, which was trying to get **vengeance** against those who had **wronged** him.

道真の怨霊を**慰める**ため、さまざまな手が打たれました。道真の罪を赦免(しゃめん)し、最高位の太政大臣にまで昇格させました。京都の北野天満宮と太宰府の太宰府天満宮では、道真を天満天神として祀りました。その後数世紀を経て、道真は**書や文化**の神様として親しまれるようになりました。

　もうひとり、平将門（不明-940）は、京都の中央政府に対し関東地方で大きな**反乱**をおこした武将です。もとは豪族どうしの争いだったものが、940年に政府を相手にした反乱と化しました。将門は関東の国府を占領し、独自の政府を置きます。自ら新皇と称し、関東を独立国にしようとしました。しかし反乱は鎮められ、将門は殺されました。将門はのちに、現代の東京にある神田明神に祀られました。

■恐山はなぜ特別な山なのですか？

　青森県北東部にある恐山は、**祈禱師**(きとうし)や仏教徒にとって神聖な山とされています。山に囲まれたカルデラ湖の湖岸には、9世紀ごろに建てられたとされる円通寺があります。湖にかけられた**橋**は、**死後の世界**への入り口を表しています。

　恐山にはまた、幼い子を亡くした両親が積み重ねた小石の山がところどころにあります。さらに、帽子と**前掛け**をつけた小さな地蔵がいくつも並び、**おもちゃの風車**が供えられています。

　毎年7月20日から24日にかけて、イタコと呼

恐山の地蔵（青森県）

They tried to **soothe** his angry spirit in several ways. He was posthumously pardoned and even promoted to the highest of court ranks in an effort to calm his anger. Kitano Shrine in Kyoto and Dazaifu Shrine in Dazaifu were dedicated to him, and he was deified as Tenman Tenjin. Over the centuries he has evolved into the benign patron of **calligraphy** and culture.

Taira no Masakado (unknown–940) led a major **rebellion** of warriors from the Kanto area against the central government. In 940 what had begun as a local conflict turned into rebellion against the government, when Masakado attacked and occupied government quarters and installed his own administrators. He attempted to make the Kanto area into an independent state, with himself as emperor. His rebellion was crushed and he was killed. He later came to be worshipped at Kanda Myojin in present-day Tokyo.

◼ What is special about Osorezan?

Mt. Osore (Osorezan) is in northeastern Aomori prefecture. The mountain is sacred to both **shamans** and Buddhists. On the banks of the caldera lake is Entsuji temple, said to date from the 9th century. There is a bridge representing the entrance to the **afterworld**.

There are also small stones piled by parents who have come to pray for the spirits of their children who died young. There are also small statues of Jizo, with caps and **bibs**, and **pinwheels**.

Mediums known as *itako* gather here July 20–24.

ばれる霊媒師（巫女）が恐山に集まります。イタコは客の求めに応じて死者の霊と交信し、その言葉を客に伝えます。しかし今では、イタコも訪れる客も少なくなっています。

🔲 天狗とはなんですか?

天狗は、日本の**民間伝承**に伝わる、鳥と人間の姿をあわせもつ生き物です。胴体と四肢は人間で、顔は赤く、背には翼が生えています。長く突き出た鼻と、極太の眉も特徴です。天狗のお面はたいてい真っ赤に塗られ、金色の目玉が描かれています。田舎の旅館や商店で、**魔除け**として売られていることもあります。

Upon request, these women communicate with the deceased. Both the *itako* and their clients are decreasing in number.

▣ What is a *tengu*?

A *tengu* is a half-bird, half-man creature from Japanese **folklore**. He has a man's body, arms and legs, a red face, and wings. He also has a long nose and brushy eyebrows. *Tengu* masks are often painted red and have eyes that glitter. They are sometimes sold at inns and shops in the countryside as **talismans**.

天狗は元来、山を守護する山の神が姿形を現したものだとされています。人々は天狗の持つ**超自然的**な力を恐れながらも、災いから守護してくれる存在だと考えてきました。また、同じく山中で暮らし修行を行う山伏と結びつけられ、しばしば山伏独特の衣装をまとった姿で描かれます。

▣ 七福神とはどのような神様ですか？

　15世紀から17世紀にかけて人気を集めた**七福神**は、ヒンドゥー教や仏教、道教の神々、そしてインド・中国・日本の**賢人**たちから成る七柱の神々の総称です。たいてい、宝船に乗った姿で描かれます。

Basically the *tengu* is the bodily form of a *yama-no-kami*, the guardian of a particular mountain. He is feared for his **supernatural** powers, but may also be seen as a protector. The *tengu* is associated with the *yamabushi*, ascetics who also live and practice rites in the mountains. Often *tengu* are shown wearing items of the distinctive costume of the *yamabushi*.

◾ Who are the Seven Deities of Good Fortune?

The Seven Deities of Good Fortune, *Shichifukujin*, became popular during the 15th through 17th centuries. They include Hindu, Buddhist and Daoist deities and **sages** from India, China and Japan. They are usually pictured riding on a treasure ship, *takarabune*.

①恵比寿	Ebisu
②寿老人	Jurojin
③大黒天	Daikokuten
④福禄寿	Fukurokuju
⑤毘沙門天	Bishamonten
⑥布袋	Hotei
⑦弁財天	Benzaiten

毘沙門天はインドを起源とする戦いの神で、怪我などの被害から守ってくれる神様です。

　大黒天もインド起源の神様です。農家や台所を守護し、洪水を防ぎます。たいてい右手には打出の**小槌**を持ち、豊作になると増えるといわれる鼠を従えた姿をしています。

　弁財天もインド起源の神様で、七福神の中で唯一の女神です。音楽や文学、芸術の神です。

　福禄寿は中国を起源とする長寿と**子宝**の神様です。しばしば瓢簞（ひょうたん）の瓶と巻き物をたずさえた姿をしています。

　布袋は中国の歴史上の人物で、幸福と充足の神様です。笑い仏ともいわれ、布袋の腹をなでると幸運が巡ってくると伝えられています。

　寿老人は中国起源の神様で、長寿と幸運をもたらします。酒のはいった瓢簞をたずさえています。

　恵比寿は日本の神様です。漁民を守護し、商売繁盛をもたらします。たいてい、めでたさの象徴である鯛を抱えた姿をしています。

Bishamonten (India) is the god of warriors and protects against harm and injury.

Daikokuten (India) protects farmers and the kitchen and prevents floods. This deity is often shown with a magic **mallet** and mice, which increase during a good harvest.

Benzaiten (India), the only female deity, is the patron of music, literature and the arts.

Fukurokuju (China) is the deity of long life and **fertility**. He is often shown with a drinking gourd and a scroll which is inscribed the wisdom of the world.

Hotei (China) is the deity of happiness and contentment. He is also called the Laughing Buddha, and rubbing his stomach is said to bring good luck.

Jurojin (China) brings long life and good fortune. He carries a drinking gourd filled with rice wine.

Ebisu (Japan) is the deity who protects fishermen, business and wealth. He is often shown with a sea bream (*tai*) which symbolizes congratulations.

Shinto

神道

伊勢神宮 風日祈宮橋(三重県)

◼ 神道は、どのようにして生まれたのですか?

神道は一般に宗教ととらえられていますが、仏教やキリスト教などのいわゆる世界宗教とは性格が異なります。神道には**創始者**がいませんし、経典がなく、体系だった**教義**もありません。

もともと神道は、自然現象や祖先、多様な神々を崇拝する古代の信仰が融合して生まれたもので、信仰に呼び名はありませんでした。しかし中国から仏教が伝来すると、仏教と古くからの信仰との区別をはかるため、「神の道」を意味する神道という名称で呼ばれるようになりました。

神道と仏教は互いに影響しあいながら共存してきました。神道の神は仏が**具現化**したものだとも考えられました。ときに、両宗教が政治的な争いの道具になったこともあります。しかし一般的には、神道は日常の暮らし、とくに農村の暮らしの中に取り込まれていきました。現在の日本人の暮らしにもその名残があるのは、ひとつには神道が前向きな考え方や清らかさ、祈願を重んじる、誰にでも親しみやすい信仰だからでしょう。

◼ 神とは、なんですか?

神の定義は容易ではありませんが、人々に畏怖の感情を抱かせる存在と考えればよいでしょう。災いも福ももたらすことのある神ですが、かならず驚くべき神秘の力を持っています。そうした力そのもの、あるいはそうした力を持つ存

◼ How did Shinto develop?

While Shinto is usually treated as a religion, it is different from most so-called world religions. It does not have a **founder**. It does not have real scriptures. And it does not have a system of **doctrines**.

Basically it evolved out of the ancient worship of unique natural phenomena, ancestors and various kinds of *kami*. This worship did not need to have a name until it was confronted by Buddhism, which was imported from China. Eventually it came to be called Shinto, "the way of the deities," to distinguish it from the newly introduced Buddhism.

Shinto existed side by side with Buddhism. Sometimes its *kami* were said to be **manifestations** of buddhas. Sometimes the two religions became involved in political conflicts. But as a general rule, Shinto continued to be an integral part of everyday life, especially in farming communities. It remains part of Japanese life, partly because it focuses on positive beliefs, purity and hopeful wishes. This makes it accessible to anyone, at any level of belief.

◼ What is a *kami*?

Defining *kami* is not easy. It is best to think of a *kami* as something that produces the emotions of awe or fear. A *kami* can be positive or negative, but it always possesses a miraculous, mysterious power. A *kami* is either the power itself or something that possesses such

在が神と見なされます。神は、英語の"god(gods)"よりも"deity(deities)"に近いものといえます。

日本の伝承には、**八百万の神**といって数多くの神々が存在します。神は大きく二つの系統に分けられます。一つは、日本の**神話**に描かれる天上と地上の神。もう一つは、自然や歴史上の人物を神格化した神や、農耕や漁、狩猟といったさまざまな生業にまつわる神です。

自然が神格化された例には、富士山をはじめとする山々や、滝、奇妙な形の岩、変わった形の木や高齢の樹木、雷や稲妻などがあります。動物では、シカやヘビ、キツネなどが神とみなされました。人物では、天満天神として祀られている菅原道真や、大権現として日光東照宮に祀られている徳川初代将軍の家康などがいます。

日光東照宮にある徳川家康の墓（栃木県）

■ 神話にはどのような神様が登場しますか？

古事記（712）は現存する日本最古の歴史書で、天地の始まりと日本誕生にまつわる神話が記されています。まず、イザナギノミコトと女神のイザナミノミコトが天に架かる橋の上から玉飾りのついた矛を海に差し入れ、引き出した矛先から滴りおちる水で島を創りました。二人はその

power. Rather than translating *kami* as "god/gods," it is safer to translate it as "deity/deities."

Japanese tradition refers to *yao-yorozu-no-kami*, which means "**myriads of deities**." But there are two main categories of *kami*. One kind is the heavenly or earthly *kami* mentioned in Japanese **mythology**. The other includes those connected with natural phenomena, those connected with historical people and those who are connected with prosperity, commerce and occupations. Farmers, fishermen, and hunters each have their own deities.

Natural phenomena that are considered *kami* are Mt. Fuji, other impressive mountains, waterfalls, peculiar rocks, unique or ancient trees, thunder and lightning. In the animal world, deer, snakes and foxes are considered *kami*. Among humans, over a period of time, the 9th-century court scholar Sugawara no Michizane became deified as Tenman Tenjin, patron saint of scholarship. The first Tokugawa shogun, Tokugawa Ieyasu, was deified as Daigongen at the Toshogu shrine at Nikko.

◼ What *kami* are mentioned in mythology?

The *Kojiki* (**Record of Ancient Matters**, 712) is the oldest existing chronicle of Japan. It records the mythology of the creation of heaven and earth and the founding of Japan. It tells how the male deity Izanagi no Mikoto and the female deity Izanami no Mikoto stood on the Floating Bridge of Heaven and stuck

島へ降りていき、夫婦として結ばれます。

イザナミはさらに日本列島の島々を創り、多くの神々を産みました。しかし、火の神を産んだときに体を焼かれて死んでしまいました。イザナギは深く悲しみ、妻を追って地下の世界、黄泉(よみ)の国へ降りていきました。見ないでほしいという妻の頼みを聞かずに、イザナギは醜くなった妻の姿を見てしまいます。慌てて逃げ出しましたが、姿を見られて怒ったイザナミが追いかけてきました。イザナギはなんとか逃げ切り、黄泉の国の出口に大きな岩をのせ、生者の世界と死者の世界を隔てました。その後、イザナギが黄泉の国でけがれた身を清めると、太陽の神であるアマテラスオオミカミと、弟のスサノオノミコトが生まれました。アマテラスは、神道の神話において中心的な役割を持つ女神となっています。

■ 神に接するときはどうすればよいのですか？

神は**恐ろしい**面も、慈悲深い面ももつ存在です。人は誠実に、正直に、**良心**をもって神に接しなければなりません。これは、「まこと」といわれる神道の基本的な信仰態度の一つです。そして神と接する前には、心身を清める必要があります。たとえば、神社の入り口では水でお清めをしなくてはなりません。

人々は自ら神にご加護を願うことも、神職に

the Heavenly Jeweled Spear into the ocean below the bridge. The water from that spear formed an island. On the island the two carried out the rites of marriage.

Izanami gave birth to the islands of Japan and their various deities. When she gave birth to the fire deity, she was burned and died. Deeply saddened, Izanagi followed her into the underworld, *Yomi no Kuni*, and found her in a terrible state. She pleads with him not to look at her. But he does, and out of shame and anger, she pursues him back to the entrance to the underworld. He barely escapes, then pushes a boulder across the entrance, separating the world of the living from the world of the dead. He carries out a purification rite which produces the Sun Goddess, Amaterasu, and her brother Susanoo no Mikoto. Amaterasu became the principal female deity of Shinto mythology.

◼ How should one approach *kami*?

Kami have both **malevolent** and beneficent characteristics. Humans must be sincere, truthful and **conscientious** when approaching a deity. These three characteristics are part of *makoto*, the essential attitude of worship in Shinto. Humans must also purify themselves before approaching, for example, by purifying themselves with water before entering the shrine grounds.

An individual may ask the deity for help or may

祈禱をとりもってもらうこともできます。ご加護が得られたら、あらためて参拝して神に感謝を表します。感謝を怠ると、神の罰である**祟り**が起こるとされています。

▣ 八幡とは、どのような神様ですか?

八幡は武士と土地の守り神です。あるとき、奈良の**大仏**の建設を守護する、という八幡のお告げが下りました。752年に大仏が完成すると、八幡は仏教の守護神とされ、大菩薩の称号が贈られました。

やがて八幡は強力な軍勢を誇る源氏の**守護**神となります。源頼朝（1147-1199）は鎌倉幕府を開くと、さらに支配力を強めたいと考え、鎌倉に八幡を祀る神社を建立しました。鶴岡八幡宮と名付けられ、東日本の代表的な八幡神社となっています。八幡神社は日本各地にあり、小さな神社も含めると、その数はおよそ3万近くあるといわれています。

鶴岡八幡宮（神奈川県）

▣ 稲荷とは、どのような神様ですか?

稲荷は、米をはじめとする穀物の神のひとつです。また、豊穣の神とされることから、商売の守護神とも考えられるようになりました。江戸時代（1603-1868）には、**商売繁盛**を願って数多くの稲荷神社が建てられました。現代では、よ

be assisted by priests. When a benefit is received, the individual should return on another occasion to express gratitude. If the individual fails to do this, he may receive **divine retribution** (*tatari*).

▣ What kind of *kami* is Hachiman?

Hachiman is revered as the *kami* of warriors and the community. An oracle announced that Hachiman would protect the construction of the **Great Buddha** (*daibutsu*) at Nara, completed in 752. From that time on, Hachiman was seen as a Shinto protector of Buddhism. The *kami* was given the Buddhist name *Daibosatsu*, meaning "Great Bodhisattva."

Hachiman became the **tutelary** *kami* of the Minamoto, a powerful military clan. When Minamoto no Yoritomo (1147–1199) established the shogunate at Kamakura, he wanted to strengthen his claim to power. He did this by building a shrine to Hachiman in the city. Named Tsurugaoka Hachimangu, it is the main Hachiman Shrine in eastern Japan. There are reported to be close to 30,000 smaller shrines to Hachiman around the country.

▣ What kind of *kami* is *Inari*?

Inari is one of the names of the deity of cereals or grains, which of course includes rice. Because *Inari* is associated with agriculture, it is also a guardian of commerce. During the Edo period (1603–1868), *Inari* shrines were built by those hoping for **prosperity and**

伏見稲荷大社の狐（京都府）

り規模の大きな産業の神ともとらえられ、企業のオフィスなどでも祀られています。小さな神社も含めると、日本には3万もの稲荷神社があるとされています。

中世の日本では、白狐が稲荷の神聖なる使いであると考えられていたため、白狐も稲荷と呼ばれるようになりました。また、**油揚げ**が稲荷と呼ばれるようになったのは、白狐の大好物だと考えられていたからだそうです。

◨ 神社とは、どのようなところですか？

神社は、閉ざされた神聖な空間です。入り口にはほとんどの場合、鳥居といわれる門が立っています。鳥居をくぐると、神社を守護する一対の犬の石像、狛犬が置かれています。狛犬は朝鮮から伝わったとされます。鳥居の正面にある建物が、拝礼をするための**拝殿**です。そのさらに奥に、神々の祀られている**本殿**があります。

拝殿の前には、参拝者がお**賽銭**を入れるための賽銭箱が置かれています。参拝者はお参りに来たことを神に知らせるため、賽銭箱の前で重たい縄をゆすって鈴を鳴らし、拍手を大きく2回打ちます。拝殿の中では、神職による祭儀が執り行われます。本殿には、神の魂が宿るとされるご**神体**が安置されています。

神社によっては、神に音楽や舞を奉納するための施設である神楽殿を備えています。

success. Today *Inari* is taken as the deity of even large companies, and head offices may have an *Inari* shrine on the property. There may be as many as 30,000 *Inari* shrines throughout Japan.

In medieval Japan, it was believed that white foxes were sacred messengers of *Inari*. The fox also came to be called *inari*. Because it was believed that the fox's favorite food was **fried soybean curd**, it also came to be called *inari*.

▣ What are the characteristics of a shrine?

Shinto shrines are enclosed sacred areas. The entrance usually has a *torii* gate. Inside the gate may be two stone *komainu* (Korean dog) sculptures that protect the shrine. The building facing the gate is a **worship hall**, *haiden*, and behind it is the **main sanctuary**, *honden*.

In front of the worship hall is a wooden box to receive **money offerings** from visitors. This is where worshippers announce that they have come to worship. They do this by pulling on a heavy rope to make a sound with the bell (*suzu*) and by making a good sound by clapping their hands, usually twice. The *haiden* is where priests carry out ceremonies and rituals. The *honden* contains the **sacred object** in which the spirit of the deity is believed to reside.

There may also be a stage or hall (*kaguraden*) for sacred dance and music (*kagura*).

神社境内図
Shrine Compound

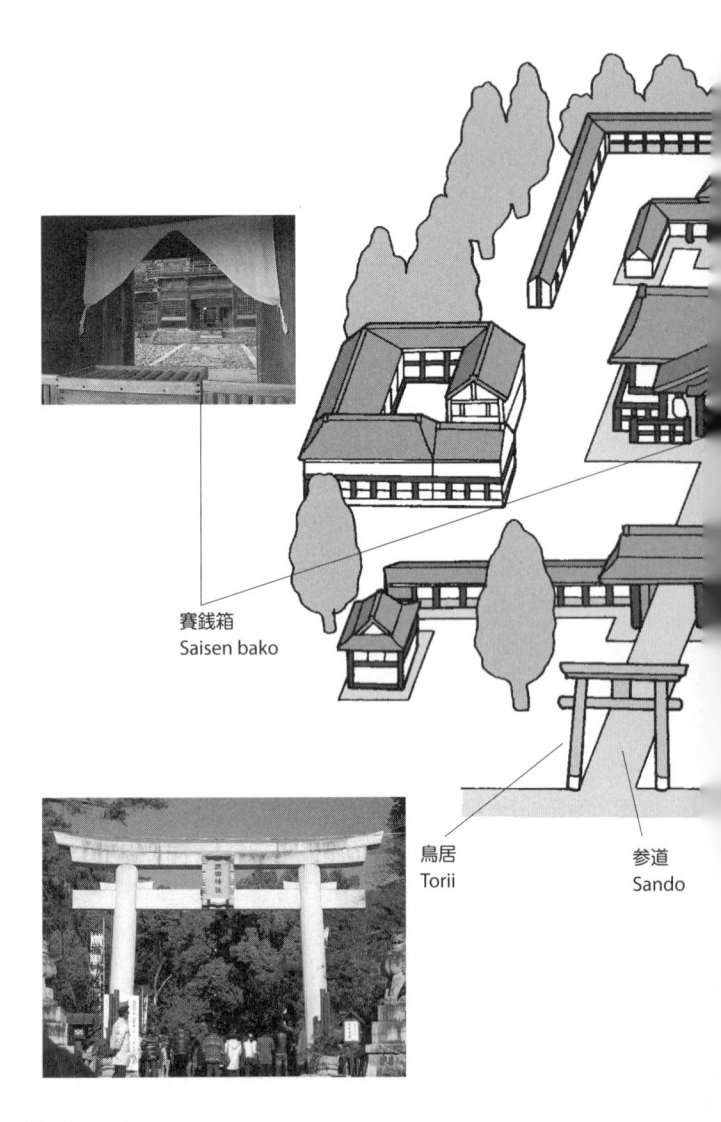

賽銭箱
Saisen bako

鳥居
Torii

参道
Sando

本殿
Honden

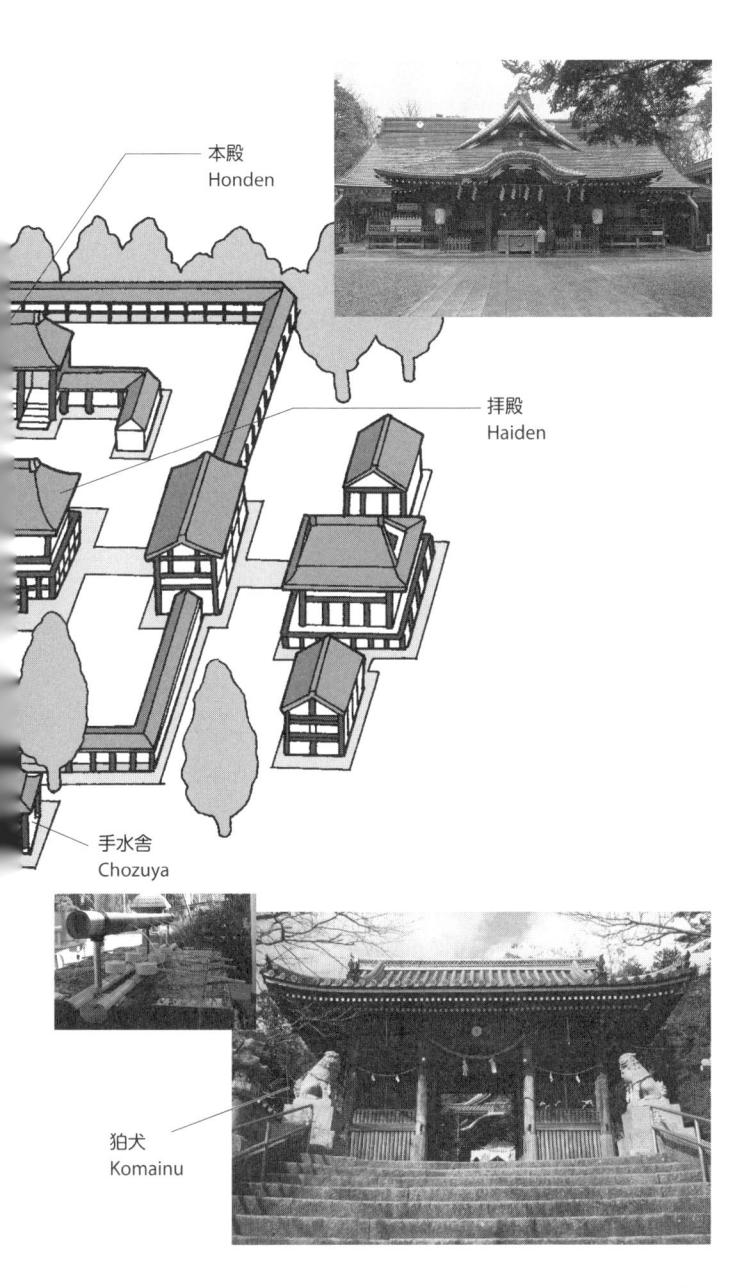

拝殿
Haiden

手水舎
Chozuya

狛犬
Komainu

Shinto ● 69 ●

日本には神社がいくつありますか？

　日本にはおよそ8万の神社があります。どの神をどれだけの神社が祀っているのかを数字でみると、それぞれの神への信仰の厚さや人気がうかがえます。最も多く祀られているのは八幡（7817社）で、その次に伊勢（4425社）、天神（3953社）、稲荷（2970社）、そして熊野（2963社）とつづきます。また同じ神様でも、地方によって信仰の厚さに違いがあります。たとえば、菅原道真を祀った太宰府天満宮がある福岡県では、天神を祀る神社が672社あるのに対し、八幡を祀る神社は245社しかありません。

神社、神宮、大社の違いはなんですか？

　神社とは、神が住まい、祭儀が執り行われる施設全般をさす名称です。神宮は、**天皇家**と関わりのある神社をさし、東京都の明治神宮や、三重県の伊勢神宮がその代表例です。大社は神社を分類する用語で、きわめて重要な神社である島根県の出雲大社がその一つです。

明治神宮（東京都）

礼拝の対象であるご神体は、神社で見ることができますか？

　神社に安置されているご神体そのものは、神ではありません。ご神体は神を象徴する神聖な事物であり、神社の本殿に納められています。ご

◼ How many shrines are there in Japan?

There are some 80,000 shrines in Japan. The number of shrines devoted to each of the *kami* indicates the degree of belief in the efficacy of each deity. The most popular is Hachiman (7,817 shrines), followed by Ise (4,425), Tenjin (3,953), *Inari* (2,970), and Kumano (2,963). Popularity is different in each region. For example, in Fukuoka prefecture, home of the Daizaifu Tenmangu shrine **dedicated** to Sugawara no Michizane, there are 672 Tenjin shrines and only 245 Hachiman shrines.

◼ What is the difference between *jinja*, *jingu* and *taisha*?

Jinja (shrine) is the overall name for places where a *kami* (divine spirit) resides and where rituals are performed. *Jingu* is the name for certain shrines that have some connection with the **imperial house**. The most famous examples are Meiji Jingu in Tokyo and Ise Jingu in Mie prefecture. *Taisha* is the term for a shrine used for Izumo Taisha, a particularly important shrine in Shimane prefecture.

出雲大社（島根県）

◼ Can you see the *shintai* (object of worship) inside the shrine?

The *shintai* in a shrine is not a *kami*. It is a sacred object that symbolizes the *kami* inside the inner worship hall (*honden*) of the shrine. This object of worship may be

Shinto

神体とされるものは、鏡や石などさまざまです。人の目に触れることはほとんどなく、本殿の建て直しなどがないかぎり取り出されることはありません。仏教の礼拝対象である**仏像**のほとんどを見ることができるのとは対照的です。

▶ 祭りとはなんですか?

祭りとは、神道由来のさまざまな儀式をさします。多くは、米の収穫祝いや地域共同体の幸福などを祈願するもので、神々や祖先の霊をもてなす神道の儀礼が起源となっています。

主な儀礼として、**五穀豊穣**（ごこくほうじょう）の祈願や神への感謝、天災や**疫病**からの守護祈願などがあります。祭りは共同体の人々と神の交わりを象徴する行事であり、共同体全体で参加し、**ご馳走**を共に食すのが一般的です。

現代では、神道とは関係のない特別な催しに対しても「祭り」という言葉を使うようになっています。

▶ 神輿とはなんですか?

神輿は、祭りが行われるあいだ神を乗せて神社の外へ運び出すための、いわば"携帯神社"で、肩に担いで運ぶものがほとんどです。大きさは、子供でも担いだり引いたりできる小さな神輿から、重さ1トン以上もある大型のものまでさまざまです。

a mirror, a stone, or something else. This *shintai* is not usually seen or taken out, except when a new building is constructed. In contrast, the **Buddhist statues** that are objects of worship at temples are on display.

◉ What is a *matsuri*?

Essentially *matsuri* (festivals) are ceremonial occasions of Shinto origin. They are chiefly related to rice cultivation and the spiritual well-being of the local community. They have their origin in Shinto rites to please the gods and the spirits of the dead.

The basic rites are prayers for a **successful harvest**, prayers of thanksgiving and prayers for the prevention of disasters or **pestilence**. These rites are symbolic acts of communication between the local people and the local *kami*. This involves the whole community and usually involves some form of shared **feast**.

The term *matsuri* is also borrowed and used to describe special events that are newly created and have no Shinto background.

◉ What is a *mikoshi*?

Mikoshi are "portable shrines" that carry the *kami* from a shrine through the streets of the community during a festival. They are usually carried on the shoulders of the participants. They range from small palanquins that children can carry or pull to huge palanquins weighing over a ton.

祭りによっては、神輿を海の中まで引き込んで担いだり、船に乗せて色々な場所を巡ったりするものもあります。

■節分とはなんですか？

節分は季節の移り変わりを示す節目のことですが、今日ではとりわけ**太陰暦の**新年がはじまる前の2月3日をさすようになりました。

毎年この時期には、「**鬼は外、福は内**」と言いながら豆まきをして、災厄をはらい、幸運を招く儀礼を行います。千葉県の成田山新勝寺をはじめとする大きな神社では、有名な相撲力士や芸能人が大勢の参拝客に向かって豆をまきます。参拝客はその豆を拾って、魔除けとして持ち帰ります。

■鳥居とはなんですか？

鳥居は、神社の**境内**の入り口に立っている門です。門の上部には横木が渡してあり、反り返ったものや真っ直ぐなものがあります。鳥居をくぐらずに境内に入ってもかまいません。

鳥居の形には、神社の社殿の建築様式に合わせた20あまりの様式があります。鳥居をよく見ると、どの神を祀った神社なのかが分かります。

平安神宮大鳥居（京都）

During some festivals, the *mikoshi* may be carried into the sea or loaded onto a boat and carried to various locations before returning to the shrine.

◨ What is setsubun?

Historically setsubun marks the change from one of the four seasons to another, but nowadays it specifically marks February 3, near the **lunar** New Year, the day before the begining of spring.

At this time every year, people throw beans to symbolically force out misfortune and bring good fortune and prosperity. They do this by saying, "Oni wa soto, fuku wa uchi," which literally means "**Demons out, good fortune in!**" At major shrines like Narita-san Shinshoji, a major temple near Narita Airport, well-known sumo wrestlers and entertainers scatter beans into crowds of visitors. The visitors take the beans home as good luck charms.

◨ What is a *torii*?

A *torii* is a gate to the entrance of a shrine **compound**. It has a crossbeam at the top, which is sometimes curved and sometimes flat. It is not necessary to walk through the gate.

There are some 20 different styles of *torii*, each matching the style of the shrine buildings. If you look at these closely you can tell which *kami* is enshrined in it.

🔲 なぜ鳥居は赤く塗られているのですか?

京都の平安神宮をはじめ、多くの神社や鳥居が赤や**朱**に塗られています。赤や朱は、邪悪なものから守護してくれる神聖な色だと考えられているためです

🔲 手水舎は何をするためにあるのですか?

神社の境内を入ってすぐのところにある小さな建物が、身を清める儀式を行うための手水舎です。屋根の下に大きな水盤が備えられ、青銅でできた龍の口や竹筒などの注ぎ口から水が流れています。参拝者は水盤のそばに用意された**柄杓**を使って、両手を洗い清めます。

◼ Why are *torii* sometimes painted red?

Some *torii* and shrines, such as Heian Shrine (Heian Jingu) in Kyoto, are painted red or **vermilion**, which are considered sacred colors that protect against evil.

◼ What is the purpose of the *chozuya*?

At the entrance to the precincts of a shrine is a small pavilion called a *chozuya*. It is "a place for ceremonial washing of the hands." It has a roof which covers a spout from which water pouts out into a broad basin. The spout is often a bronze dragon's mouth or a bamboo pipe. There are usually several long-handled **ladles** for worshippers to use. You rinse your hands with water from the ladle as a symbolic purification.

①柄杓を右手に持ち、左手に水をかけます。
First, take the ladle in your right hand, and pour water over your left hand.
②柄杓を左手に持ち替え、右手に水をかけます。
Switch hands and pour water over your right hand.
③ふたたび右手で柄杓を持ち、左手で受けた水を口に含みます。
Switch hands again, and pour water over your left hand again and then into your mouth
④最後にもう一度柄杓に水を満たし、逆さに立てて柄に水をかけ流します。
Take water into the ladle one more time, raise the scoop end and let the water flow down the handle toward you.
⑤元の位置に戻します。
Put it back.

まず、柄杓を右手に持ち、左手に水をかけます。次に柄杓を左手に持ち替え、右手に水をかけます。ふたたび右手で柄杓を持ち、左手で受けた水を口に含みます。このとき、柄杓をじかに口にあててはいけません。口をすすいだら、排水用の溝に水を吐き出します。最後にもう一度柄杓に水を満たし、逆さに立てて柄に水をかけ流します。こうして次に使う人のために柄杓の柄を清めておきます。

▣なぜ参道沿いに石灯籠が並んでいるのですか?

石灯籠は大きな石造の灯籠で、神社の本殿や寺院の本堂へつづく道の両脇に置かれています。元来は、神事などが行われる際に蝋燭や灯油の火がともされていましたが、現代では電灯を使うことが多くなりました。石灯籠は神社や寺院を支援する個人や企業から寄贈され、たいてい**寄贈者**の名前が刻まれています。

奈良県の春日大社の参道沿いには2000もの石灯籠が立ち並び、実に壮観です。

春日大社の石灯籠(奈良県)

▣なぜ神社や寺院の参道には砂利が敷かれているのですか?

神社や寺院につづく参道には通常、**玉砂利**が敷かれています。玉砂利には神聖な場所の周辺を清め、邪悪な霊を寄せ付けない作用があると考えられています。また、玉砂利の上を歩くと足

First, take the ladle in your right hand, and pour water over your left hand. Switch hands and pour water over your right hand. Switch hands again, and pour water over your left hand again and then into your mouth, without putting your lips directly to the dipper. Empty the water from your mouth in front of the trough. Take water into the ladle one more time, raise the scoop end and let the water flow down the handle toward you. This purifies the handle, and makes it clean for the next person who uses it.

◾ Why are there stone lanterns (*ishi-doro*) along the path to a shrine?

Ishi-doro are large **stone lanterns** that are placed on both sides of the path or road leading to the main building of a shrine or temple. Originally they held a candle or an oil lamp, lit for special occasions. Nowadays, many are lit by electricity. They are gifts from individuals and companies who support the shrine or temple. Usually the name of the **donor** is written on the lantern.

The most impressive *ishi-doro* are the 2,000 that lead to the Kasuga Shrine in Nara.

◾ Why are the *sando* leading to shrines and temples laid with gravel?

The *sando*, "approach to a shrine or temple," is often covered with **gravel**. Gravel (*tamajari*) is believed to purify the ground around sacred places. It prevents evil spirits from entering. People make noise when they

音が鳴るので、断りなく入り込もうとする者をしりぞける効果もあります。

なお、参道を歩くときは道の真ん中ではなく、端を歩くのが礼儀正しい作法とされています。

🔲 注連縄とはなんですか？

注連縄は、稲藁の束を縒り合わせた縄に白い紙垂を取り付けたものです。神聖な領域を示す役割をもち、邪気や病を**追い払う**力があると考えられています。

出雲大社の注連縄（島根県）

注連縄は神社の周辺にある特別な木や岩に巻きつけたり、神社の入り口に飾ったりします。なかでも有名なのは、島根県の出雲大社の神楽殿に飾られている巨大な注連縄です。全長13メートル、周囲9メートル、重さは5トンにもなります。

また、特別に編まれた白い注連縄は、大相撲の横綱が儀式で身につける欠かせない装飾品のひとつです。

🔲 紙垂は何に用いるのですか？

紙垂は、稲妻形に切り整えた紙を注連縄に垂れ下げるものです。神社に神が宿っていることを示すため、注連縄に下げたり、柱に垂らしたりします。また、木の串や神事で用いられる榊の枝にとりつけることもあります。御幣に取りつける紙垂は主に白い紙で作られますが、金色の紙や

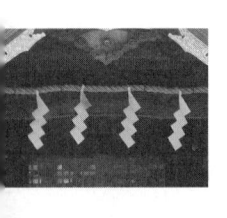

walk on gravel, so it also discourages people who try to enter without permission.

Incidentally, it is considered more proper to walk toward the side of the path rather than right down the middle.

◼ What is a *shimenawa*?

A *shimenawa* is a rope made of twisted strands of rice straw. When decorated with white paper, it marks a sacred space. It is believed to have the power to **ward off** evil and sickness.

A *shimenawa* may be placed around a distinctive tree or rock, especially within the area surrounding a shrine. One may be placed at the entrance to a Shinto shrine. The most well-known is an enormous *shimenawa* that hangs before the kaguraden of Izumo Taisha in Shimane prefecture. It is 13 meters long and 9 meters in circumference. It weighs 5 tons.

In professional sumo a Grand Champion wears a specially tied white *shimenawa* as an essential part of his outfit in certain ceremonies.

◼ What are *kamishide* used for?

Kamishide are zigzag strips of paper. They indicate the presence of a deity at a shrine. They may hang from a piece of rope or a vertical post. They are also attached to a wooden stick or to a branch of sakaki that is offered to the *kami* in formal rites. Most *kamishide* are made of simple white paper, while others are made of special

綿布、あるいは**金メッキをした金属板**で作られるものもあります。

▣ 拝殿につるしてある鈴は何に使うのですか?

多くの神社では、賽銭箱の上に、上からつるされた鈴が結わえつけられた太い縄が垂れています。参拝者はその縄を振って鈴を鳴らし、神に呼びかけます。さらに、**手を打ち鳴らす**拍手を行い、自分が参拝にきたことを神に知らせます。

▣ 神楽とはなんですか?

神楽とは、神を**慰め**喜ばせるための神聖な音楽や仮面の舞をさします。大きな神社で行われるほか、地域の祭りや皇室の儀式においても演じられます。神楽の始まりは、遅くとも9世紀ではないかとされています。現代では、日本の**民俗芸能**の一つとして考えられています。

▣ 拍手とはなんですか?

神社では、手を叩いて音を鳴らす拍手は神の注意を引くための礼儀正しい作法です。参拝に訪れたら、神に知らせる必要があると考えられています。

伊勢神宮での正しい拝礼の方法は、まず深く2回礼をし、胸の高さで拍手を大きく2回打ちます。そして手を合わせてお祈りをし、最後に1回、深く礼をします。神社によって、拍手を3回打ったり、4回打ったりするところがあります。明治

gold paper, cotton cloth or **gilt metal**.

▣ What are the bells used for?

Above the wooden box for offerings at many shrines is a thick rope connected to a bell. People shake the rope to make noise with the bell in order to call the deity. Making a sound by **clapping the hands together**, called *kashiwade*, is another part of making your presence known to the deity.

▣ What is *kagura*?

Kagura, sacred music and masked dance, is performed at major shrines to **pacify** and entertain the deity. It is also performed as part of local festivals and at rituals at the imperial court. It dates from at least the 9th century. It is now considered part of Japanese **folk performing arts** (*minzoku geino*).

▣ What is *kashiwade*?

At shrines, *kashiwade*, or "clapping hands together," is the proper way of getting the attention of the deity of a shrine. It is considered necessary to announce to the deity that you have come to worship.

At Ise Shrine, the proper way to worship is to make two deep bows, make two loud claps of the hands at chest height, pray with hands together and make a final deep bow. Other shrines may call for three or four claps. At Meiji Shrine, you bow twice, clap twice and

④最後に1回、深く礼をします。
Make a final deep bow.

②胸の高さで拍手を大きく2回打ちます。
Make two loud claps of the hands at chest height.

③手を合わせてお祈りをします。
Pray with hands together.

神宮では、最初に礼を2回、拍手を2回、最後に礼を1回行います。

なお、仏教寺院では拍手を打ちません。

■お賽銭にはどのような意味があるのですか？

神社や寺院には、賽銭箱といわれるはしご状の蓋がついた木の箱が置かれています。この箱に、神に供える金銭を意味するお賽銭を入れます。新年の初詣でをはじめ、参拝の際にお賽銭を奉納し、神に祈願します。

お賽銭に決まった金額はありませんが、語呂のよい金額を入れるが多いようです。たとえば

①まず深く2回礼をします。
Make two deep bows.

bow once again.

At Buddhist temples, one does not clap.

■ What is the purpose of *osaisen*?

In front of the main hall of shrines and temples is a wooden box with a grill on top, called a *saisen-bako*. Visitors throw coins or bills into it as an offering, when they pray for something, especially at the beginning of the New Year.

There is no set amount for an offering, but people often use a kind of word play to set the amount. A large

2951（ふくこい）円なら、金額は高いですが「福よ、来い」という願いが込められています。もっと一般的なのが5円玉です。5円はご縁の**語呂合わせ**で、「神仏と絆を結ぶ」という意味もあるそうです。

◾️どうすれば神主（神職）になれるのですか？

村の小さな神社には、祭儀を執り行う専門の神職がいない場合もあります。代わりにその土地の代表者が神職を務めたり、何人かで当番制を組んだりして執り行います。

大きな神社には、専門の大学で神道を学び、訓練を受けた神職がいます。神道を学べる主な大学は、東京の國學院大學と、伊勢神宮の近くにある皇学館大学の2校です。大学を卒業後、神社で奉仕をしながら数年間勉強を続けます。一人前の神主になるには、試験に合格しなければなりません。

神職は位に応じて異なる色の袴を身につけます。基本色は白で、位に関わらず身につけられます。その次に高位の色は水色で、最も多くの神職が身につける色です。最高位の色は紫で、これより上の位は、袴に刺繍される紋章の違いによって区別されます。

烏帽子
Eboshi

笏
Shaku

浅靴
Asagutsu

donation of ¥2,951 (which could be read as *fu-ku-ko-i*) could be offered with the wish "Good luck, come!" (*fuku koi*). A much more common donation would be a single ¥5 (*go-en*) coin. The **word play** here is that *go-en* could also mean "having a bond with the deity or buddha."

◉ How does one become a Shinto priest (*kannushi*)?

The *kannushi* who performs rites at a small local shrine may not be a professional "priest." He may actually be just the headman of a village. In some cases, village leaders take turns performing that role.

At major shrines the priests are trained and are professionals. A person trains for becoming a Shinto priest by studying at a Shinto university. The two main universities are Kokugakuin in Tokyo and Kogakkan near Ise Shrine (in Mie prefecture). After graduating, the person serves for several years at a major shrine. To become fully qualified, a candidate has to pass an examination.

Ranks of Shinto priests are indicated by their *hakama*, loose trousers worn over a kimono. The basic color is white, which is worn by all priests when rank is not an issue. The next higher rank is indicated by light blue, and this is the most common color. The next higher rank is purple. From there on, ranks are shown by different kinds of embroidered crests.

千早
Chihaya

緋袴
Hibakama

◼ 巫女とはなんですか？

巫女は2種類に分けられます。古代の巫女は、霊的な呪術力を持つ女性で、神の力を呼び起こして神の**お告げ**を伝え、祖先の霊との対話をとりもつ力があるとされました。恐山に集まるイタコは、古代の巫女が起源とされています。

現代の巫女は、祭儀を執り行う神職の補佐や、神社での雑務を担う女性をさします。神道の祭りや儀式では、4人の巫女による神楽舞を見ることもできます。通常は白衣に赤い袴をはいていますが、神事の際にはその上に千早をはおり、菊などをあしらった簪をつけます。

◼ 神道の結婚式とはどのようなものですか？

神道の結婚式（神前式）では、新郎新婦は礼装用の和服を着て式に臨みます。新郎は黒い着物と袴を身につけ、新婦は白無垢を着て、角隠しといわれる白い布で頭を覆うのが伝統的な装いです。角隠しには、角に見立てた新婦の嫉妬心を抑え、隠す意味があるといわれています。

神前式にはごく近しい親類や友人のみが参列します。式の中心となるのが、三三九度と呼ばれる夫婦の契りを固める杯事です。天皇家の婚礼において行われたのが始まりとされています。三三九度では、新郎新婦が三つの杯で三度に分

◼ What is a *miko*?

There are two kinds of *miko*. In ancient times, a *miko* was a woman who possessed special magical powers. She could call forth the divine power of the *kami* and announce **oracles** from the *kami*. She could also help the living communicate with their dead ancestors. The mediums called *itako*, who gather at Mt. Osore, come from this tradition.

The contemporary *miko* is a woman who assists the priest of a shrine in ritual and clerical duties. During Shinto festivals and ceremonies, you may see four *miko* performing a dance. They usually wear a white kimono and loose red trousers called *hakama*. They may also wear a special form of cassock (*chihaya*) with chrysanthemums as a headdress.

◼ What is a Shinto wedding like?

In the Shinto wedding rite, the bride and groom wear formal kimono. Traditionally, the groom wears a black formal kimono and *hakama*. The bride wears a white formal kimono and a white *tsunokakushi* head covering. The Japanese word literally means "horn-hiding." This covering is intended to suppress and hide the bride's "horns of jealousy."

The ceremony is attended only by close family and friends. The highlight is the ceremony of exchanging nuptial cups, which originated in the households of the nobility. In the "three-three-nine times" exchange, called *sansankudo*, they take turns sipping sake from a

けて酒を飲みます。その後、玉串といわれる神聖な榊の枝を神前に捧げます。

かつて結婚式は、新郎の自宅で執り行われるものでした。しかし現代では、実際に神社で行われるほか、式後にそのまま披露宴を行える結婚式場やホテルでの挙式が好まれています。

神前式は仏教式やキリスト教式にくらべて一般的な形式でしたが、よりお洒落とされるキリスト教式が、信仰に関わらず大きな人気を集めるようになっています。

■初宮参りとは、なんですか?

初宮参りとは、家族が子どもの誕生を神に奉告するため、初めて子どもを連れて神社を参拝することをいいます。男の子は生後32日目に、女の子は33日目に初宮参りをするのが風習です。古くは、産後しばらくは母親の身体が**けがれ**ていると考えられていたため、父親と父方の祖母が子どもと神社に参拝しましたが、現代では母親も付き添う場合がほとんどです。

初宮参りでは、神職による祝詞（のりと）や巫女の舞が献上され、子どもの健やかな成長を祈願します。

set of three shallow cups. They then offer a branch of sacred sakaki on the altar.

In the past, wedding ceremonies were held in the home of the groom. But nowadays the ceremony is held at an actual Shinto shrine, in wedding halls or in special Shinto-design chambers within a hotel. The latter makes it easier to carry out the ceremony and proceed immediately to the *hiroen*, a reception attended by a larger group of friends and associates.

Shinto weddings are more common than Buddhist or Christian ceremonies. However, Christian ceremonies have become fashionable, even among non-believers.

▣ What is *hatsu miya mairi*?

A **child's first visit to a shrine** is called *hatsu miya mairi*. It is the first time that a family presents the child to the *kami* of a shrine. The first visit by baby boys is the 32nd day after birth. The first visit by baby girls is the 33rd day. In the past, childbirth was considered to leave the mother in a condition of "**impurity**." Therefore, the child's father and grandmother presented the child to the *kami*. Nowadays, the mother usually participates.

Rites during this visit include **prayers** chanted by a priest, a dance performed by a *miko* and a blessing of the child.

◼神職はどのように人々のけがれを清めるのですか?

人生の大事な局面において神のご加護を得たいときなどに、神社で神職によるお祓いを受けます。神職が祓詞といわれる祝詞を唱え、祓串を振ってけがれを清めます。

祓串

祓串は木の棒の先にコウゾの木の繊維で作った和紙を垂らしたもので、水を象徴しています。祓串を参拝者の頭上で大きく振ることで心身のけがれが洗い清められ、神に受け入れられるようになると考えられています。

◼祟りとはなんですか?

祟りとは、人間の悪い行いに対して神が罰や戒めとしてもたらす災いをさします。祟りが起こったときには、前述のようなお祓いをしなければなりません。

◼厄年とはなんですか? 災いを避けるにはどうすればよいですか?

厄年は、不幸や災難がとりわけ身に降りかかりやすいとされる年齢のことです。女性は19歳、33歳、61歳、70歳が厄年で、33歳は最も注意すべき大厄とされます。男性は、25歳、42歳(大厄)、61歳、70歳が厄年です。厄年を迎えたら神社にお参りし、災いを防ぐためにお祓いを受けて神

◼ What does a priest do to purify someone?

To gain the protection of a deity—especially during a critical period—a worshipper can have a priest perform a purification ceremony. This includes the chanting of a Shinto **prayer of purification** (*harae kotoba*) and the waving of a *harae-gushi* over the persons to be purified. It may also include the presentation of an offering to the deity.

The *harae-gushi* is sacred mulberry paper attached to a stick. This wand-like device represents water. Waving this back and forth over a person is believed to purify the person. This makes the person acceptable to the deity.

◼ What is *tatari*?

Tatari means "**misfortune**." It comes as a punishment or as a warning from a *kami* that is angered by something a human has done or said. It requires purification by a ritual like that described in the section above.

◼ What is *yakudoshi*? How do you avoid danger from it?

Unlucky years, *yakudoshi*, are ages when a person is most likely to experience misfortune or danger. For women, the ages 19, 33 (especially), 61, and 70, and for men, the ages 25, 42 (especially), 61, and 70 are considered especially critical. To avoid misfortune during these potentially risky years, some Japanese

のご加護を祈る風習があります。

◧ 祝詞とはなんですか?

祝詞は、神前において唱えられることばで、神に捧げるための独特の言い回しで語られます。言葉には霊力が宿るという**言霊**の思想から生まれたものです。祝詞には、感謝を表すものや、加護を願うもの、祈りを捧げるものなどさまざまな種類があります。現代では、神職が自ら祝詞を作ることはなく、19世紀以降に整えられた**定型文**を唱えるのが一般的です。

◧ 神社にはどのように参拝すればよいですか?

まず、手水舎で手を洗い、口をすすぎます。そして拝殿の前に立ち、お賽銭を**賽銭箱**に入れます。続いて、礼をして拍手を打ちますが、神社によって少しずつ違いがあります。伊勢神宮では、2回深く礼をし、拍手を2回打ったあと、手を合わせて祈り、最後に1回深く礼をします。神道では、拍手を打ち鳴らして神を呼び出すのが正しい作法とされています。

拝礼を終えたら、**社務所**でお守りや絵馬を買い求めることができます。

◧ 黄泉の国とはどのようなところですか?

古代の神道では、黄泉の国は死者が暮らす暗

go to shrines to have a priest perform a purification ceremony to protect them during the dangerous year.

▣ What are *norito*?

Norito are a kind of Shinto prayer. They are sacred forms of speech used when speaking to the deities during shrine rites. They are based on the idea of *koto-dama*, which means the **soul or energy of words**. Some express gratitude. Some ask for protection or a blessing. Some are prayers for individuals. Nowadays priests do not compose their own but use the *norito* in **standard collections** from the 19th century.

▣ How do you worship at a shrine?

First, at the *chozuya* you rinse your hands and mouth. Go to the main hall (*haiden*) and drop a coin in the **offering box** (*saisen-bako*). The next step is slightly different at each shrine. At Ise Shrine, for example, you make two deep bows, clap your hands twice, pray with your hands pressed together, then make one final deep bow. Other shrines call for three or four claps. This clapping, called *kashiwade*, is believed to be the proper way to get the attention of the deity of the shrine.

On your way out after worshipping, you may buy a talisman or an *ema* plaque at the **shrine office**.

▣ What is *yomi no kuni* like in Shinto?

In ancient Shinto, *yomi no kuni*, or the afterworld,

黒の世界だと考えられていました。しかし黄泉の国は現世とつながっていて、生きている人間と死者は互いに対話ができるとされました。神道には死後に人を罰するという考え方がないため、仏教やキリスト教の「地獄」とは性格が異なります。

現代では、黄泉の国の存在を信じている日本人はほとんどいません。

▣ 神社ではどのような供物を捧げるのですか？

神のご加護を願うため、神社ではさまざまな**供物**を神に捧げます。米や魚介、野菜、果物、菓子、酒などの飲食物を主に供えます。

神事においては、玉串といわれる紙垂のついた榊の枝を捧げます。参拝者はそれぞれ玉串を一本ずつ、神前の台の上に供えます。

玉串

▣ けがれとは何ですか？

けがれは、「**不純**」、「**不潔**」、「**不浄**」などの状態を意味し、出産や月経、病や死などが原因になるとされています。目に見える汚れではなく、観念上の汚れを表す言葉です。罪を負っている状態とも異なります。

また、けがれは本人の家族や周囲の人間にも

was considered a place of darkness and the realm of the dead. But the afterworld was connected with the realm of the living. People in the realm of the dead and the realm of the living could communicate with one another. In Shinto there is no idea of punishment after death, so *yomi no kuni* is different from "hell" found in Buddhism or Christianity.

Today, very few Japanese believe in an afterworld.

◘ What kind of offerings do people make at shrines?

Offerings are made to the deities to create a sense of goodwill and beneficence in the deity. Common **offerings** include food, sweets, fruit and even small bottles of sake.

In a formal ceremony, a common offering is a **sprig** of sakaki leaves, called *tama-gushi*, which has strips of paper attached to it. In a ritual led by a priest, each participant puts one sprig on a small table set up before the symbol of the deity.

◘ What is *kegare*?

Kegare refers to different kinds of "impurity," "pollution" or "**defilement**." *Kegare* is caused by child-bearing, menstruation, disease and death. It is considered to be "a feeling of uncleanliness or impurity." This is not the same as having committed a sin.

These "impurities" affect the individual and people

移ると考えられています。けがれをそのままにしておくと祟りが起こるので、**お祓い**を受けてけがれを取り除かなければなりません。

■清めの儀式であるお祓いや禊はどのように行われるのですか？

けがれはお祓いによって取り除くことができます。神との交流において求められる清浄さを**取りもどす**ことが、お祓いの目的です。心が清らかであれば、正しい行いができると考えられています。

お祓いの方法には主に3種類あります。一つめは、清めの対象となる人や場所の前で**玉串**を振る方法。二つめが、水によるお祓い、禊です。古くは、海や川、滝の下で禊が行われ、塩水には特に浄化作用があるとされました。現代では、参拝の前に手を洗い清める所作として、禊が広く浸透しています。三つめは、食事や言動を**慎む**こと（忌み）によって心身を清める方法です。

土地や建物などを清めるときには、塩をまくか、打ち水をします。よく料亭や飲み屋の玄関の両脇に、塩を小さな山のように盛った盛り塩がしてありますが、これは清めというよりも客を呼ぶためのまじないとしての要素が強いようです。

葬儀に参列して帰宅する際は、家に入る前に玄関先で自分に塩をかけます。こうすることで、

around the individual, including family members. If *kegare* is ignored, then a misfortune (*tatari*) may occur as a warning. In order to eliminate *kegare*, one should perform a **purification ritual**.

◉ How is "purification" (*oharai* or *misogi*) carried out?

A person can remove impurities (*kegare*) by purification (*oharai*). The purpose of purification is to **restore** purity, which is the basis of communion with the deities. When the heart, or *kokoro*, is pure, then all of one's actions become proper.

Purification can be done in three different ways. First, a priest can symbolically purify a person or place by waving a **wand of paper streamers** (*tama-gushi*). Second, one can purify oneself using water (*misogi harai*). In the past, people did this in the sea, in a river or under a waterfall. Saltwater was considered particularly effective. The most common form today is done by washing one's hands with water before entering a shrine. A third way to purify one's self is by **abstaining** and fasting (*imi*).

A place can be purified by scattering salt on it or sprinkling it with water. Some restaurants and bars place two small piles of salt, called *morishio*, outside the door to their business, one on each side. This custom is less to purify than to welcome customers.

Participants in a Buddhist **funeral service** may sprinkle salt on themselves before entering their home.

死のけがれが家の中に入らなくなると考えられています。

また、**お線香**の煙をからだに浴びるのもお祓いの一種です。

◾ 夏越の祓とはなんですか？

夏越の祓は、毎年6月30日に行われる伝統的なお祓いの儀式です。1年の前半6ヵ月のけがれをすべて清め、心身とも健やかに残り半年を過ごせるように祈ります。明治神宮では、6月に夏越の祓を、大晦日（おおみそか）には年越しの祓を行います。

夏越の祓では、拝殿の前に茅の輪といわれる茅萱（ちがや）でできた大きな輪が置かれます。参拝者はその輪の中を**左回り**、**右回り**、左回りとあわせて3回くぐり、幸運と健康を願います。

夏越の祓（京都府）©中田昭

◾ 人形（ひとがた）とはなんですか？

紙や木で人間の姿形を表した人形または形代は、清めの儀式で使われる道具です。人間のけがれを**人形**に移し、川へ流したり燃やしたりしてけがれを取り除きます。

◾ 日本語の"罪"は西洋における"sin"と同義ですか？

日本語の"罪"はたいてい英語で"sin"と訳されますが、まったく同じ意味ではありません。

This is believed to prevent the "pollution" of death from entering the home of the mourner.

A less common form of purification is by waving the smoke of **incense** over the body.

◉ What is *Nagoshi-no-harae*?

This is a traditional Shinto purification ceremony. It is held on June 30 each year. All the impurities of the first six months are purified. This allows participants to have a fresh start and good health for the second half of the year. At Meiji Shrine, these purification ceremonies are held on June 30 and December 31.

A ring of thatch, called a *chinowa*, is placed in front of the shrine. Visitors walk through it three times: **counter-clockwise, clockwise** and counter-clockwise again. This is believed to bring good fortune and good health.

◉ What is *hitogata*?

Cut-out paper and wooden figures of human beings, called *hitogata* or *katashiro*, are used in Shinto purification rites. The "impurities" of humans are transferred to these **effigies**, which may be thrown into a river or burned in order to take away the impurities.

◉ Is *tsumi* the same as the Western idea of "sin"?

The Japanese word *tsumi* is often translated as "sin" in English. However, "sin" includes two factors: intention "sin"は、掟を破ろうとする意図と破る行為そのものを意味するのに対し、罪はもっと**曖昧で**幅広い意味を持っています。

罪は、不潔、**心の不浄**、病、災害や過ちとも言い換えられます。人間の力ではどうにもならない事を罪ととらえることも少なくなく、そこに罪を犯す「意図」はありません。罪が人の意思と関係なく起きたことであれば、人は道義的な責任を負わないのです。

▣ 絵馬とはなんですか?

絵馬は、社務所で売っている小さな木の飾り板です。元来は、生きた馬を神に奉納していた古代の風習の名残で、その名のとおり馬の絵が描かれていました。

現代の絵馬は、神社の名前にくわえ、**干支(えと)**など多様な絵柄が描かれています。絵馬の裏側は無地になっていて、そこに神への**願い事**を書きます。**学問の神様**、菅原道真を祀る京都の北野天満宮や東京の湯島天神には、入学試験を控えた学生が大勢訪れて絵馬を買い求めます。絵馬の裏には志望校への合格祈願を書き、絵馬掛けに吊るして奉納します。

and the breaking of a moral standard. *Tsumi* is more **ambiguous** and broader in meaning.

Tsumi could be translated as impurity, **spiritual pollution**, sickness, disaster or error. Many of these experiences are beyond human control. A person does not "intend" to do these things. The events just happen, and the person is not morally responsible for them.

▣ What is an *ema*?

Ema are small wooden plaques sold at shrine offices. The word *ema* originally meant "picture of a horse," and the plaques actually had a horse painted on them. This reflects an ancient custom of offering a horse to the deities of certain shrines.

Present-day *ema* have the name of the shrine and some unique design on it. The design may be the current year's animal according to the **Chinese zodiac** or a design of the shrine. The back is blank so that people can write a **petition** to the shrine's deity for assistance in achieving some objective. Kitano Tenmangu (Kyoto) and Yushima Tenjin (Tokyo) enshrine the spirit of Sugawara no Michizane, the **patron of learning**. Students preparing for entrance exams often visit this shrine and buy one of the *ema*. They write their hopes for success in getting into a good school on the back and hang it on the racks that are placed for that purpose.

◼ お御籤とはなんですか? 何が書いてあるのですか?

お御籤は中国から伝来した古い慣習で、未来を予言する**神のお告げ**をくじ引きするものです。神社だけでなく、寺院でもお御籤を引くことができます。くじ引きの方法は主に二つあります。印のついた棒が入った箱を振って1本取りだし、印によってお御籤と引き換える方法と、お御籤の入った箱から直接引く方法です。このように無作為にお御籤を選び出す方法は、神仏による**導き**を意味しています。新年の初詣での際には、多くの日本人がお御籤を引きます。

お御籤は細長い紙を小さく畳んだもので、大吉から凶までいくつもの段階に分かれた運勢が書かれています。また、願い事や恋愛、旅行、病気、仕事など生活のさまざまな面での運勢も個別に記されています。

引いたお御籤を神社の木の枝や専用のお御籤掛けに結びつける習慣もあります。お御籤を結びつけると、幸運を招き災厄を防いでくれると考えられています。大吉のお御籤を引いたときには、**お守り**として家に持ち帰ります。

◼ お札とはなんですか?

お札とは、神社や寺院の名前と神仏の名前が書かれた木の守り札のことで、主に縦長の五角形の形をしています。お札は神様の**分身**と考え

◼ What is an *omikuji* and what does it tell you?

The drawing of *omikuji*, **oracle** lots that predict the future, is an ancient custom that came from China. These paper lots are commonly found at both Buddhist temples and Shinto shrines. Lots may be drawn by shaking a stick out of a container and using the mark on the stick to select a fortune written on paper. Or a lot may be drawn directly from a box. Either way, this random selection is understood to be the **guidance** of the buddhas or deities. Japanese often draw lots at the beginning of the year.

Actual *omikuji*, literally "sacred lots," are long rolled-up strips of paper. Each has one of a dozen or so overall oracles, such as *daikichi* (great blessing or great fortune), *kichi* (blessing or fortune), *kyo* (curse or bad fortune) and *daikyo* (great curse or worst fortune). Each also foretells specific aspects of life, including hopes, romance, travel, illness and business.

Some people tie their paper lot on a tree branch or on wires provided by the temple or shrine. They may hope this will make a good fortune come true or prevent bad luck from occurring. Those who draw a good luck lot may take theirs home as a **charm**.

◼ What are *ofuda*?

Ofuda are flat pieces of wood, slightly broader and pointed at the top. On them are written the name of the shrine (or temple) and the deity (or buddha) that

Shinto ● 105 ●

お札

られ、ひとつひとつ白い紙で包んで紐で結ばれています。家内安全のお守りとして、家庭で祀ります。

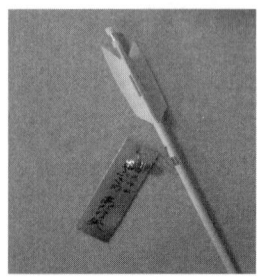

🔲 破魔矢とはなんですか?

破魔矢は、邪悪を打ち破る矢を意味し、古くは邪悪な霊から守護する魔除けとして考えられていました。現代では、家族に健康や福をもたらすお守りとして、一年の始めに初詣での参拝客が買い求めるようになりました。

破魔矢

🔲 お守りとはなんですか?

お守りには、不幸をしりぞけ、災難から守護してくれる効力があると考えられています。たいていは袋の口を紐で結んだ小さなお守り袋に納められており、中を見てはいけ

お守り

ないとされています。袋の中には、文字や経文が記された紙などが入っています。袋の表には神社や寺院の名前が記され、裏には何に効くお守りなのかが記されています。主なものには、健康や**家内安全**、交通安全、**商売繁盛**、**安産**などを祈願するお守りがあります。小学生が背負うランドセルによくお守りがぶらさがっています。

is worshipped there. *Ofuda* are considered *kamisama no bunshin*, an **incarnation** of the deity. Each *fuda* is wrapped in a white paper and tied with string. It is placed in the home in order to protect the house and its surroundings.

▣ What are *hamaya*?

Hamaya are "evil-destroying arrows." In the past they were believed to protect against evil spirits. Nowadays they are considered a charm that brings good health and well-being to members of the family. These arrows are available in early January when people make their first visit of the year to shrines.

▣ What are *omamori*?

Omamori are **amulets**. They are believed to prevent misfortune and to protect a person against danger. An *omamori* is usually a small cloth pouch with drawstrings. You are not supposed to look inside the pouch. Inside is a piece of paper with an inscription or piece of scripture. On the outside is the name of the shrine or temple, with the benefit on the reverse side. There are usually amulets for good health, **household safety** (*kanai anzen*), transportation safety (*kotsu anzen*), **financial success** (*shobai hanjo*), and **safe birth** (*anzan*). You will often see one of these on a child's school satchel or backpack.

Shinto ● 107 ●

■ 熊手とはなんですか？

熊手には幸運や客を「かき集める」という意味が込められており、伝統的に飲食業者の間で人気があります。めでたさを象徴する鈴や商売繁盛の神様、**米俵**、金貨、鶴、亀などを豪勢に飾りつけた大きな熊手が、古くから飲食店などで縁起物(えんぎもの)として扱われてきました。

日本各地の大鳥神社で11月に開かれる酉の市では、熊手を売る露店が立ち並びます。酉の市は、その年の曜日の並びによって11月に2回、または3回開かれます。

■ へのこ祭、おそそ祭とはどのようなお祭りですか？

へのこ祭り（男根の祭り）は愛知県小牧市にある田県神社の祭事で、おそそ祭り（女陰の祭り）は隣接する犬山市の大県神社の祭事です。ともに、五穀豊穣と子孫繁栄を祈願する祭りです。田県神社にある**男根**をかたどった像に女性が触ると、子を授かりやすくなるといわれています。大県神社には女陰を象徴する石が祀られ、**夫婦円満**と**子授け**、豊作のご利益があるとされています。

■ 三種の神器はどこにあるのですか？

三種の**神器**は、皇族の象徴である神聖な宝器です。神話には、太陽神アマテラスより三種の神

▣ What are *kumade*?

A *kumade*, "bear's paw," is an ornamental rake. It is supposed to "rake in" good luck, wealth and customers, so it is popular among traditional drinking establishments and restaurants. Large rakes are decorated extravagantly with auspicious symbols of bells, deities of prosperity, **bales of rice**, gold coins, cranes, and tortoises.

Markets selling these *kumade* are held at Otori Shrines on festival days in November. There are two or three festival days, called *Tori-no-ichi*, depending on the year.

▣ What are the Henoko Matsuri and Ososo Matsuri?

The Henoko Matsuri, or Phallus Festival, is held at Tagata Shrine (near Nagoya). The Ososo Matsuri, or Vagina Festival, is held nearby at Oagata Shrine (near Inuyama). These festivals are held to protect harvests, cure sterility and guarantee success. If a woman touches the sacred objects, the **phalluses**, at the Tagata Shrine, it is supposed to encourage pregnancy. At Oagata Shrine, the clam, which is a symbol of the vagina, is supposed to guarantee **marital harmony**, **pregnancy** and a good harvest.

▣ Where are the *sanshu no jingi*, the three imperial regalia?

The three **imperial regalia**, *sanshu no jingi*, are sacred objects that symbolize the imperial family. It is held

Shinto

器を授かった孫のニニギノミコトが、日本の島々を治めるために天上より降臨したと記されています。

三種の神器は、八尺瓊勾玉（やさかにのまがたま）、草薙剣（くさなぎのつるぎ）、八咫鏡（やたのかがみ）の三点をさします。八尺瓊勾玉は、皇居に三つある神殿のひとつ、賢所に納められているとされます。草薙剣と八咫鏡の所在には諸説ありますが、剣は熱田神宮に、鏡は伊勢神宮に安置されているのではないかと主に考えられています。

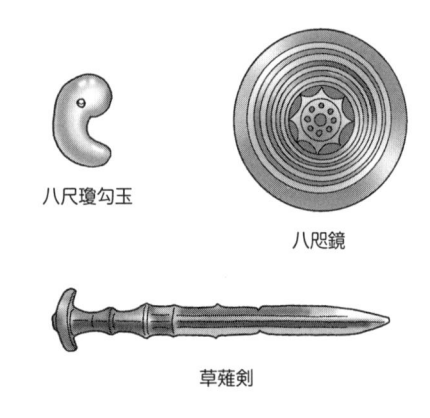

八尺瓊勾玉

八咫鏡

草薙剣

◼ 伊勢神宮（三重県伊勢市）

二つの正宮（しょうぐう）と複数の神社で構成される伊勢神宮は、日本で最も重要な神社の一つです。3世紀に建てられた内宮（ないくう）には、三種の神器のひとつである八咫鏡をご神体とするアマテラスが祀られています。

5世紀に建てられた外宮（げくう）には、衣食住の守り神であるトヨウケノオオカミが祀られています。

that these three objects were given by the Sun Goddess, Amaterasu, to her grandson, Ninigi no Mikoto, when he descended from heaven to rule the Japanese islands.

The three sacred objects are curved jewels, a sword and a mirror. The curved jewels, *yasakani no magatama*, are said to be kept in the Kashikodokoro, "the Place of Awe," which is one of the three shrines in the Imperial Palace in Tokyo. The sword, *kusanagi no tsurugi*, is said to be kept at Atsuta Shrine in Nagoya. The mirror, *yata no kagami*, is said to be stored at Ise Shrine.

▣ Ise Shrine (Mie prefecture)

The complex at Ise is considered one of the most important Shinto shrines in the country. The Inner Shrine, *Naiku*, was established in the 3rd century and it enshrines Amaterasu, who is represented by a sacred mirror. The mirror is considered one of the three sacred regalia.

The Outer Shrine, *Geku*, was established in the 5th century and it enshrines Toyouke no Okami, the god

正宮をはじめ主要な各社殿の隣には何も建っていない土地があり、20年に一度、その土地に神殿が建て替えられます。もとの社殿は取り壊され、次回の建て替えを行うための敷地になります。定期的に建て替えを行う伝統は、**自然の再生力**への信仰に基づくものでもあります。

◼ 江戸時代、伊勢神宮への巡礼が突如盛んになったのはなぜですか？

江戸時代、おかげ参りと呼ばれる伊勢神宮への集団参拝がおよそ60年周期で流行しました。「伊勢に天から護符が降ってくる」という噂が**きっかけになった**といわれます。1705年には350万人もの人々が伊勢神宮に参拝したとされ、多くの人々が無断で仕事などを放り出し、伊勢を目指したそうです。

◼ 出雲大社（島根県出雲市）

出雲大社は日本で最も古く、最も重要な神社の一つです。祭神は、**縁結びの神、福の神、農耕の神**として慕われています。とりわけ縁結びの神社として大きな人気を誇り、若い女性は良縁を祈るために、恋人同士は愛が続くように祈るため、参拝に訪れます。社殿に飾られている大注連縄は、恋人同士を結ぶ縁結びの象徴でもあります。

現在の本殿も高さ24メートルとじゅうぶんに

of food, clothing and housing.

Next to each of the main shrine buildings is an empty lot. Every 20 years, these buildings are rebuilt on the adjacent lot. The old shrine is taken down and the space is left for the next rebuilding. The regular rebuilding is part of a belief in the **renewal of nature**.

◉ Why were there sudden pilgrimages to the Grand Ise Shrine during the Edo period?

Spontaneous mass thanksgiving pilgrimages to the Grand Ise Shrine, called *okage mairi*, occurred roughly every 60 years during the Edo period (1600–1868). They **were touched off** by rumors that sacred amulets, *gofu*, were falling from heaven at Ise. In 1705, some 3.5 million people are reported to have made such a pilgrimage. The majority simply dropped everything and left without preparation or official permission.

◉ Izumo Taisha Shrine (Shimane prefecture)

Izumo Shrine is one of the most ancient and important shrines in Japan. The deity is regarded as protecting marriage, good fortune and agriculture. It is one of Japan's most popular shrines related to *enmusubi*, **making or strengthening marital relationships**. Young women visit the shrine praying to find a husband. Young couples visit it to pray that their relationship will last. The "tying of couples" is symbolized by an enormous *shimenawa* that hangs before the shrine.

The current shrine (24 meters high) is large enough,

大きいものですが、**考古学者**たちによれば、上古には高さ96メートルもの巨大な本殿が建っていたといいます。

日本では旧暦の10月を神無月といいます。この時期には日本各地の神々が出雲に集まって話し合いをすると考えられたためです。一方、出雲地方では旧10月を神在月と呼び、神在祭を行います（神々が出雲へ出かけているあいだは、台所の神である恵比須が留守を守るとされています）。このことからも、出雲が古来よりいかに重要な地であったかがうかがえます。

◼ 明治神宮（東京都渋谷区）

1912年に明治天皇が亡くなった後、1920年に建てられたのが明治神宮です。高さ12メートルもの大きな鳥居が立てられています。本殿には、明治天皇と昭憲皇太后の御霊(みたま)が祀られています。第二次世界大戦中に焼失しましたが、1958年に再建されました。初詣での参拝先として日本一の人気を誇り、毎年**正月三ヵ日**には300万人以上が訪れます。

◼ 熱田神宮（愛知県名古屋市）

熱田神宮には、三種の神器のひとつである草薙剣が安置されていると考えられています。

but **archaeologists** believe that the ancient shrine was absolutely enormous (96 meters).

The ancient name for October in other parts of Japan was "month without deities" or *kanna-zuki*. It was believed that the *kami* from all over the country gathered at Izumo to confer about their local regions. Therefore, in mid October Izumo Shrine celebrates with the *Kamiari matsuri*, a festival "with deities present." (While the deities are at Izumo, the deity who protects the kitchen stove, Ebisu, takes over). The name and the festival symbolize just how important Izumo was in ancient times.

▣ Meiji Shrine (Tokyo)

Emperor Meiji died in 1912 and Meiji Shrine was built in 1920. The great *torii* is 12 meters in height. The main hall, *honden*, is dedicated to the spirits of Emperor Meiji and Empress Shoken. The building was destroyed during World War II and rebuilt in 1958. The shrine is one of the most popular places for *hatsumode* in Tokyo, visited by more than three million during the **first three days of the year**.

▣ Atsuta Shrine (Nagoya)

This shrine is said to house *kusanagi no tsurugi*, the "grass-cutting sword," which is one of the three imperial regalia.

◨ 湯島天神（東京都文京区）

天神を祀る神社は日本全国にあり、教育にたずさわる人々から厚い信仰を集めています。湯島天神にはとりわけ大勢の受験生が参拝に訪れ、学力向上や試験合格の祈願を託した絵馬が数多く奉納されます。

◨ 鶴岡八幡宮（神奈川県鎌倉市）

八幡は、日本の北東部を征した源氏の**氏神**でした。源頼朝は鎌倉に**幕府**を開くにあたり、この絢爛（けんらん）な神社を建立し、源氏の守護神として八幡を**祀り**ました。

拝殿へつづく石段の脇には、樹齢1000年ともいわれる有名な**銀杏**（いちょう）の大木が立っていましたが、強風のために根元から折れて倒れてしまいました。しかし、折れた幹の一部を植え直したところ、見事に芽を吹き返しました。

鶴岡八幡宮は、馬を走らせながら矢を射る**流鏑馬**が見られる神社としても有名です。流鏑馬は年に2回、4月の第3日曜日と9月16日に行われます。

◨ 日光東照宮（栃木県日光市）

日光東照宮は、徳川幕府を開いた徳川家康を主祭神とする神社の一つです。1873年に、豊臣秀吉と源頼朝が合祀されました。豪華絢爛な社

◉ Yushima Tenjin (Tokyo)

Tenjin shrines around the country are popular among people involved in education. Yushima Tenjin is particularly popular among students who are preparing for entrance exams to the next level of schooling. The requests that visitors write on the *ema* that they leave at the shrine are often pleas for help in studying well and in passing the examinations.

◉ Tsurugaoka Hachiman-gu (Kamakura)

Hachiman was the **clan deity** of the Minamoto clan which conquered the northeast part of Japan. When Yoritomo established the **shogunate** at Kamakura, he had this magnificent shrine built to **enshrine** his clan's protector.

The shrine was long known for a 1,000-year-old **ginkgo** tree that stood by the stairway leading up to the shrine. Unfortunately the tree was recently destroyed in a storm, but efforts have been made to cultivate an offshoot of the original tree.

Tsurugaoka Hachiman Shrine is one of the most famous places to see *yabusame*, **archery on horseback**. This is held twice a year, on the third Sunday of April and on September 16th.

◉ Toshogu (Nikko in Tochigi prefecture)

Toshogu is dedicated primarily to Tokugawa Ieyasu, the founder of the Tokugawa shogunate. Since 1873 it is also dedicated to Toyotomi Hideyoshi and

殿と門は、家康の遺体を祀るために1636年に建て替えられたものです。家康を祀る東照宮は、日光のほか日本各地に建立されています。

■平安神宮（京都府京都市）

平安神宮は比較的新しい神社で、1895年に平安遷都(せんと)1100年を記念して建てられました。大極殿には平安京で過ごした最初と最後の天皇（桓武天皇と孝明天皇）が祀られています。平安神宮の社殿は平安遷都当時の建築を模したもので、中国の影響を受けた建築様式で建てられています。

■伏見稲荷大社（京都府京都市）

伏見稲荷大社は、五穀豊穣の神、稲荷を祀る神社です。全国に大小合わせて約3万ある稲荷神社のなかで、総本社とされています。もとは稲荷山の峰に神を祀っていましたが、のちに山の麓に社殿が移され、同じく京都にある真言宗の総本山、東寺の守護神社となりました。また、千本鳥居といって、およそ1万もの朱色の鳥居が立っていることでも有名な神社です。

初詣での参拝先として、西日本では最も大きな人気を集める神社の一つです。とりわけ、**商売繁盛**のご利益があるといわれています。

Minamoto no Yoritomo. The ornate shrine and gateways were built in 1636 for Ieyasu's remains. Branch shrines exist throughout the country.

◼ Heian Shrine (Kyoto)

Heian Shrine is unique partly because it is comparatively new. It was built in 1895 to mark the 1,100th anniversary of the founding of the capital at Kyoto. The Daigoku-den enshrines the spirits of the first and last emperors to reside in Kyoto. The shrine is in Chinese architectural style because it was meant to resemble the original buildings in that style, when the capital was first established and the called Heian Capital.

◼ Fushimi Inari Taisha (Kyoto)

Fushimi Inari Taisha in Kyoto is dedicated to *Inari*, the deity of cereals, which of course includes rice. This shrine is one of the most important of the 30,000 Inari shrines among registered religious organizations. It was originally built at the foot of Mt. Inari (*Inariyama*). It was moved to Fushimi so its deities could protect Toji, the major Shingon Buddhist temple nearby. It is famous for the hundreds of vermilion *torii* that one passes through on the way up to the shrine.

It is one of the most popular shrines in western Japan to visit during New Year's. It is held to be especially suitable for prayers for **prosperity and success in business** (*shobai hanjo*).

◾葵祭とはどのような祭りですか？

葵祭は、毎年5月15日に、京の朝廷の守護神社とされた上賀茂神社と下鴨神社で行われる豊作祈願の祭りです。祭りの日の朝、平安時代の**貴族**の衣装を身につけた人々が**京都御所**に集合します。御所を出発して下鴨神社、上賀茂神社へと巡り、両神社で祭儀を行います。その後、ふたたび御所へ戻ります。

◾祇園祭とはどのような祭りですか？

祇園祭は7月1日から約1ヵ月にわたって八坂神社で行われる祭りです。なかでも最大の見どころは、7月17日に行われる山鉾巡行です。長い**鉾**を立てて飾りつけた山鉾といわれる山車が、街中で引き回されます。祇園祭の起源は、平安時代初期の866年にさかのぼります。京都を疫病が襲った際、当時の日本にあった国々を表す鉾を八坂神社の境内に立て、疫病の蔓延が収まるよう祈りを捧げたのが始まりとされています。

◾厳島神社（広島県廿日市市）

厳島神社は、日本で最も美しい場所のひとつとされています。漁師や船乗りの守護神が祀られ、創建は593年と伝えられています。厳島は島そのものが神として崇められていたため、神社は島の上ではなく、島の縁の入り江に建てられました。14世紀になるまで、島に人が住むこと

◼ What is the Aoi Festival?

The Aoi (Hollyhock) Festival is held on May 15 in Kyoto to pray for a good harvest. It is held at the Kami-gamo and Shimo-gamo shrines. These are the protector shrines of the palace and the (former) capital. On the morning of the festival, participants dressed like Heian period **nobles** gather at the **Kyoto Imperial Palace**. They proceed to Shimo-gamo Shrine and Kami-gamo Shrine where they hold rites and ceremonies. They then proceed back to the palace.

◼ What is the Gion Festival?

The Gion Festival is held in July. The main event is on July 17. On that day, floats (*dashi*) decorated with spears parade through the streets. The festival began in 866 when a plague struck Kyoto. Tall **spears** (*hoko*) representing each province of Japan were set up at Yasaka Shrine. Prayers were offered to stop the epidemic that was spreading across the city.

◼ Itsukushima Jinja (Hiroshima prefecture)

Itsukushima Shrine is considered one of the most scenic places in Japan. The shrine is dedicated to the deities who protect fishermen and seamen. According to tradition, it was established in 593. The island itself was considered sacred, so the shrine was not built on the island itself, but on the water's edge. Until the 14th

は禁じられ、神社の神職でさえ対岸に住んでいたといいます。

厳島神社の代名詞ともいえるのが、島から沖合160メートルほどに立つ大鳥居です。**クス**の木で造られた鳥居は、1875年から変わらずに立っています。もう一つ大きな特徴は、多くの社殿が水中に組んだ土台の上に建てられていることです。それぞれの社殿は**回廊**で結ばれています。満潮時には、神社が海に浮かんでいるように見えます。境内にはまた、舞楽や能を演じるための舞台も備えられています。

■地鎮祭や鍬入れは何のために行うのですか？

地鎮祭とは、字のとおり土地を守護する氏神の怒りを鎮める祭事を意味し、建設地を清めるための儀式です。建築工事を始める前に執り行います。

一般的には、土地の四隅に立てた青竹のまわりに注連縄を張りめぐらし、儀式のための神聖な空間を創ります。その中に**祭壇**を設け、酒や米、塩、魚などの供物を奉納します。

鍬入れは、はじめてその土地に鍬を入れる着工の儀式です。たいていは神職が、工事の始まる前に鍬入れを執り行います。また農村では、新年の仕事始めの儀式として田畑で鍬入れを行うこともあります。

century, no one was allowed to live there. Even the shrine priests lived across the bay.

The shrine is unique because its *torii* gate is 160 meters or so out in the bay. The gate is made of **camphor** and has survived since 1875. Also unique is the fact that many of the shrine buildings are also built on pillars in the bay. They are connected by **corridors**. When the tide rises, it seems like the shrine is floating on the water. There are several stages: one for *bugaku*, court dance and music, and one for Noh.

◼ Why do people perform *jichinsai* and *kuwaire*?

Jichinsai is a ceremony that purifies a building site. Literally a "ground-calming festival," it is intended to pacify the local guardian deities (*ujigami*). It is carried out before any turning over of the soil.

Generally, four poles of green bamboo are set up in a square. They are tied together with straw rope to create a sacred space for the ritual. In the space, an **altar** is set up. On the altar are placed offerings of such things as sake, water, rice, salt and fish.

Kuwaire is a groundbreaking ceremony. Usually a Shinto priest performs the ceremony in which a **hoe**, or *kuwa*, is used to break the ground before construction of a house or a building begins. At New Year's some farming communities perform the ceremony in a selected field.

■建築中の家屋についている豪華な飾りはなんですか?

破魔弓は神事で使われる弓矢で、屋根の一番高い棟木(むなぎ)に飾られます。鬼門(きもん)である北東からやってくる災いを弓矢が打ち落とし、工事中の職人と完成した家屋に住まう人を守護するとされています。地方部でより多く見られる風習です。

■神棚とはなんですか?

神棚は家庭で神を祀るための棚です。神社との結びつきを生み、祖先の霊を拝むために設けられます。

米・塩・水・酒を、毎日または月に2回供えます。また、神社で授かったお守りやお札なども納めます。自分の職業にまつわる神様や、住んでいる土地の氏神を併せて祀ることもできます。

神棚は家庭のほかにも、料亭や鉄道駅舎、会社事務所、酒造所などをはじめ、とりわけ日本の伝統産業にかかわる店舗や職場の多くで設けられています。

◾ What are those elaborate decorations on the houses under construction?

Hamayumi are ceremonial Shinto bow-and-arrow figures. Carpenters construct them at roof-raisings. It is believed they will "shoot down" any misfortune that might come from the northeast, an **unlucky direction**. This protects the carpenters during the construction and the people who will live in the house. These are more common in the provinces.

◾ What is a *kamidana*?

Sometimes called a "god shelf" in English, the *kamidana* is a Shinto altar in the home. It is used to connect the household with a shrine and to honor the spirits of the ancestors.

Offerings of rice, salt, water and sake may be made daily or twice a month. Some people put amulets or *ofuda* from shrines on the altar. The altar may enshrine a deity that protects a particular occupation and also protects a district.

Small altars can also be found in Japanese-style restaurants, railway stations, company offices and sake breweries. This is especially true among more traditional trades and occupations.

▣ 門松とはなんですか？

門松は、3本の青竹と松の枝を縄ひもで束ねた一対の飾りで、新年を迎えるころから家やオフィスビルの入り口の両側に立てられます。

門松は神が依りつく物を意味する依り代の一つです。新年に訪れる**歳神様**の宿る場所として門松を飾り、神を迎えます。たいてい1月7日に取り払われ、神社の境内で燃やされます。さまざまな正月飾りを燃やす祭事のなかでも、仙台の大崎八幡宮で行われるどんと祭は全国的に知られています。

▣ 鏡餅とはなんですか？

鏡餅とは歳神様に奉納するための大きな平たい丸餅で、杵と臼を用いた餅つきによって作られます。この丸餅を二つ重ねたものを、さまざまな正月飾りと一緒に神棚など神前に供えます。

▣ 初詣でとはなんですか？

初詣でとは、新年が明けて初めて神社や寺院にお参りをすることです。**大晦日**の真夜中に、有名な社寺に参拝することも珍しくありません。正月三ヵ日のうちに初詣でを済ませるのが一般

◼ What is a *kadomatsu*?

Kadomatsu is a pair of decorations made of three pieces of bamboo and pine branches tied together with straw. They are placed in front of houses and office buildings at the end of the year.

The *kadomatsu* is a seasonal type of *yorishiro*, literally "approach substitute." Its purpose is to attract the *kami* with a place to reside during the New Year season. In this case, people want to attract *Toshigami-sama*, the **deity of the new year**. Usually on January 7 the decoration is taken down and placed in a ritual bonfire at a shrine. One well-known ceremony in which New Year's decorations of various kinds are thrown onto a bonfire is the *Donto-sai* at the Osaki Hachiman Shrine in Sendai (Miyagi prefecture).

◼ What is *kagami-mochi*?

Kagami-mochi are large, **round cakes of rice**. They are made from steamed glutinous rice which is pounded in a wooden mortar with a large wooden mallet. These big flat cakes are made as an offering to *Toshigami-sama*, the god of the new year. They are set on altars with other auspicious New Year decorations.

◼ What is *hatsumode*?

Hatsumode, "the first shrine or temple visit," refers to a person's first visit of the New Year. It is common for Japanese to visit well-known shrines or temples beginning at midnight on **New Year's Eve**. Often,

的です。

湯島天神(東京都)

明治神宮や鶴岡八幡宮、川崎大師、八坂神社には、とりわけ大勢の初詣で客が訪れます。

■ 相撲と神道は関係があるのですか?

相撲の起源は、農作物の豊凶を**占う**古代の神事にあるとされます。現代の大相撲においても、土俵の吊り屋根の四隅から垂れる**房**や、力士の塩まき、いくつかの儀式などに神道の要素を見てとることができます。

土俵の屋根はもともと4本の柱に支えられていましたが、現在では吊り屋根となり、柱の名残（なごり）として房を垂らすようになりました。4本の房のうち、青い房は東方の守護神である青竜と春を表し、赤い房は南方を守護する朱雀と夏を、白い房は西方を守護する白虎と秋を、黒い房は北方を守護する玄武と冬を表しています。

各場所が始まる前には、土俵を清めるための神事が行われます。また**取り組み**の際には、**力士**は水で口をゆすいで身を清めてから土俵に上がり、塩をまいて土俵を清めます。

新たに**横綱**に昇進した力士は、明治天皇を祀る明治神宮で土俵入りの型を見せる儀式を行います。毎年春には、横綱と大関らが伊勢神宮に参拝します。

however, people make this visit sometime during the first three days of the year.

Especially popular are Meiji Shrine (Tokyo), Tsurugaoka Hachiman Shrine (Kamakura), Kawasaki Daishi (Kanagawa) and Yasaka Shrine (Kyoto).

◉ Is *sumo* part of Shinto?

Sumo has been traced to ancient harvest **divination**. Certain elements in contemporary professional *sumo* are related to Shinto, such as the roof over the ring and its **tassels**, the throwing of salt, and certain other rituals.

The roof was once supported by four pillars, but they are now represented by tassels. The green tassel represents spring and the green dragon god of the east (*seiryo*). The red tassel represents summer and the red sparrow god of the south (*shujaku*). The white tassel represents autumn and the white tiger god of the west (*byakko*). The black tassel represents winter and the turtle god of the north (*genbu*).

The ring, or *dohyo*, is purified in a Shinto ceremony at the beginning of each tournament. Prior to a **bout** (*torikumi*) and before entering the ring, each **wrestler** (*rikishi*) purifies himself by rinsing his mouth with water. He then purifies the ring by throwing salt into it.

All newly promoted **Grand Champions**, *yokozuna*, perform a formal ritual at Meiji Shrine, which honors the spirit of Emperor Meiji. The *yokozuna* and other top-ranked wrestlers also pay respects at Ise Shrine each spring.

■ 国家神道とはなんですか?

国家神道は本物の宗教ではありません。宗教の要素を用いて、中央集権的に国家を管理しようとした試みをさします。**明治維新**後、新政府は神道の思想や組織、儀式を利用し、天皇を現人神とする思想と日本の独自性・優位性を主張する国体思想を国に広めました。これにより、神社は国の行事が行われる場となり、**行政組織**の一部になりました。神社は、国民に愛国心と忠誠心を持たせるための施設になったのです。神職らは政府から任命されるようになり、国民は神社への信仰を義務づけられました。

第二次世界大戦後にこの体制は解体されました。現代の神社は民間の宗教組織ですが、靖国神社などいまだ行政とのつながりがみられる神社も一部存在します。

■ 靖国神社の何が問題なのですか?

東京の靖国神社には**戦没者**が祀られています。靖国神社をめぐる論争の発端は、1979年に、東条英機をはじめとする**A級戦犯**がその前年に合祀されていた事実が公表されたことでした。以降、歴代首相の多くが靖国神社に参拝しました。ほとんどの場合、一個人として参拝するのか、首相としての**公の立場**で参拝するのかは曖昧にされてきましたが、1985年、当時の中曽根首相は首相として公式に参拝したことを明言しました。

◼ What was "State Shinto," *Kokka Shinto*?

"State Shinto" was not a true religion. It was an attempt to centralize government administration, using religious elements. Beginning with the **Meiji Restoration**, the new government made use of Shinto ideas, organizations and ceremonies. It encouraged two beliefs: the divinity of the emperor and the uniqueness of Japan's "national essence," or *kokutai*. It turned shrines into places for national ceremonies. In other words, shrines became **government institutions**. The main purpose of the shrines was to foster patriotism and loyalty. Priests were appointed by the government and citizens were required to register with local shrines.

After World War II, this system was abolished. Today shrines are private religious organizations. But shrines like Yasukuni Shrine still appear to have a semi-government character.

◼ Why is there controversy about Yasukuni Shrine?

Yasukuni Shrine (Tokyo) enshrines the **war dead**. The main issue surrounding the shrine began in 1979. In that year it was made known that **Class-A war criminals**, including Prime Minister Tojo Hideki, had been memorialized the year before. From that year onward, various prime ministers visited the shrine. They usually did not say whether they did this as private citizens or **as public officials**. In 1985, Prime Minister Nakasone announced that he visited the shrine as a

近隣諸国の政府は、靖国神社の公式参拝は日本軍と日本の歴史を称える行為だとして懸念を示しています。一方で擁護する側は、あくまで戦没者を悼(いた)む行為だと主張しています。この論争は今もなお続いており、簡単には解決しそうにありません。

靖国神社(東京都)

government official.

Some foreign governments see this as promoting the military and praising Japan's past. The opposition says that this is just **honoring** the dead. The issue continues and will not be easily settled.

Connections between Shinto and Buddhism

神道と仏教のつながり

青岸渡寺五重塔と那智の滝（和歌山県）

◼ 神社と寺院が同じ場所に建っていることがあるのはなぜですか?

7世紀に仏教が日本で広まってまもなく、日本人は仏と神を結びつける方法を模索しはじめました。まず、土地を守護する氏神が仏教の守護神として考えられるようになりました。10世紀には、神は仏や**菩薩**が姿を変えて現れたものであるとされ、13世紀になると主要な神社の祭神の多くが、特定の仏の化身として同一視されるようになりました。

こうした神仏の同一視から生まれた思想が、**本地垂迹**です。仏が日本の神々の姿をとって地上に降りてくることを意味しています。仏教を守護する菩薩としても崇められる八幡はその代表例です。寺院の境内に神社が建てられたのは、神道と仏教を一つにまとめるためでした。このことは、単一の宗教にこだわらず、複数の宗教を受け入れる日本人の信仰のあり方をよく表しています。

◼ なぜ神道と仏教は切り離されたのですか?

江戸時代、寺院は徳川幕府によって行政組織に組み入れられ、**住民登録**を請け負う役所と化しました。国民は住所によって割り当てられた寺院に登録しなければなりませんでした。寺院は政府による国民統制の一端を担うことになったのです。結果として、仏教は本来の活力を失い、その役割は葬儀や法事を行うことが中心になり

🔲 Why are a shrine and a temple sometimes found in the same place?

When Buddhism was introduced to Japan in the 7th century, Japanese almost immediately began to try to find a way to relate buddhas and deities. The local *kami* were seen as protectors of Buddhism. By the 10th century, Shinto deities were taken to be incarnations of buddhas and **bodhisattvas**. By the 13th century, deities of many major shrines were identified with particular Buddhist deities.

Out of this developed the concept called *honji suijaku*, "**original essence, descended manifestation.**" This means that Shinto deities are Japanese manifestations of buddhas. The best example is the Shinto deity Hachiman, who was taken to be a bodhisattva protecting Buddhism. Shrines were built at temples bringing the two religions together. This "cooperation" is an example of how Japanese tend to accept multiple forms of religion, rather than choosing just one.

🔲 Why were Shinto and Buddhism completely separated?

During the Tokugawa period, the government turned Buddhist temples into government agencies. Temples became **public registrars**. Each person in a specific neighborhood was required to "register" as a member of the local temple. Therefore, the temples served as a kind of government office for controlling the citizens. As a result, Buddhism lost its vitality during this period.

ました。1868年には、神道と仏教を区別するためとして、明治新政府により**神仏分離**令が発布されました。

▣ なぜ明治時代に反仏教運動が起きたのですか？

江戸時代、徳川幕府は寺院を利用して国家統制を強めました。力を持つようになった寺院に対し、人々は不満を募らせていました。しかし明治時代になると、新政府は寺院から特権を奪い、かわりに天皇制支配を支える思想として神道を利用しました。そうしたなか、神道の信奉者らによって引き起こされたのが**廃仏毀釈**運動です。歴史ある寺院や**経巻**、仏像など重要な美術品が日本各地で破壊されました。運動は1871年に終息しましたが、以来ずっと両宗教は分離したままです。

▣ 現代の日本人は、仏教もしくは神道を信仰しているのですか？

文部科学省は宗教に関する**統計調査**を毎年行なっていますが、その結果は驚くべきものです。2006年度の調査によると、神道の**信者数**は1億500万人、仏教の信者数は8900万人でした。合計すると1億9400万人になりますが、当時の日本の総人口は1億2600万人です。これは何を意味するのでしょうか？

Instead, it became primarily associated with funeral ceremonies for members. The new Meiji government in 1868 ordered the **separation of Buddhism and Shinto**, which is known as *shinbutsu bunri*.

◉ Why was there an anti-Buddhist movement during the Meiji period?

During the Tokugawa period, the government used the Buddhist temples for its own purposes. Many ordinary people resented the power that the temples and priests seemed to have. The new Meiji leaders took this power from the Buddhist temples. These leaders instead began to use Shinto as a way of supporting leadership under the emperor. Using the slogan "**eradicate Buddhism**," *haibutsu kishaku*, some Shinto followers destroyed priceless Buddhist temples, **sutras** and works of art. This anti-Buddhist period ended in 1871, and the two religions remained separate from then on.

◉ Are Japanese today believers in Buddhism or Shintoism?

The **Statistical Survey** on Religion carried out annually by the Agency of Cultural Affairs reveals amazing statistics. According to the 2006 survey, there are more than 105 million **adherents** of Shintoism and 89 million adherents of Buddhism in Japan. These numbers do not include the other religions. However, in that year the Japanese population was only 126 million. How is this possible?

そもそも、上記の信者数に数えられている人々は、自分が神社や寺院に属している意識すらないかもしれません。この信者数は、個人ではなく神社や寺院が提供した数字です。つまり、仏教との接点が葬儀や法事だけの人でも、檀家として名を連ねていれば仏教信者として数えられているのです。

　統計結果からは、日本人が同時に複数の宗教と関わりを持っていることが分かります。日本人は概して信仰に熱心ではないと言えるかもしれません。ただ、さまざまな宗教や伝統に対して寛容であることもまた確かでしょう。

Actually, the people counted as "adherents" may not even be aware that they "belong" to a shrine or temple. The number of registered members is provided by the shrines and temples, not by individuals. All members of a temple *danka* are counted, even though the only connection individuals might have with the temple priest involves a funeral.

The numbers suggest that Japanese simultaneously hold several religions at one time. It is safer to say that most Japanese are not actively involved in religious activities. It is also safe to say that they are open to various religious traditions.

Buddhism

仏　教

延暦寺根本中堂（京都府）

■ 仏教とはどういうものですか?

ゴータマ・シッダールタは「釈迦族の聖者」として釈迦牟尼とも呼ばれており、その生年は紀元前4世紀から5世紀の間となっています。シッダールタは釈迦族の王子としてぜいたくに育てられ、老、病、死といった辛さや悲しみを伴うもの一切に触れることがないよう守られていました。しかしながら最終的には、人間の生にあるこうした忌むべきものすべてを見出してしまいます。

シッダールタは剃髪し、**悟り**を求めて出家しました。ヒンドゥー教の導師らとともに数年間の**苦行**を積んだ後、インド北西部のガヤにあった**菩提樹**の下で瞑想し、悟りに達します。根本の真理、それは人生が**苦**であるということ。人間の苦は、老いていくこと、欲しいものが得られないこと、愛する人と別れることなどいろいろな原因から生じるものなのだ。シッダールタはそう悟りました。

釈迦は「悟れる者」として仏陀と呼ばれるようになり、人々に説法を始めます。自身を苦しみから解き放つには「**四聖諦**(四つの聖なる真理)」を理解せねばならないと仏陀は説きました。その四つとは苦という真理、苦の原因という真理、苦の滅という真理、苦の滅を実現する道という真理です。この「悟り」を得るために、人はすべての欲望、そしてこの世への**執着**を滅せねばなりません。これは日々**瞑想**し、精神的な鍛錬を行い、**教え**に従うことによって為し得ます。仏陀は

◼ What is Buddhism?

Gautama Siddharta is also called Shakyamuni, "sage of the Sakya clan." He was born in the 4th or 5th century B.C. As the son of the king of the Sakya clan, he was raised in luxury. He was protected from everything that was depressing, including aging, illness and death. Eventually, however, he discovered on his own all of these unpleasant and disturbing facts about human life.

He shaved his head and set off in search of **enlightenment**. After years of **ascetic practice** and study with Hindu masters, he meditated under a **bo tree** near Gaya, in northeast India, and attained enlightenment. He realized the fundamental truth is that life is **suffering**. Our suffering comes from different causes such as growing old, not having something we want, and parting from someone we love.

Shakyamuni came to be called the Buddha, "the Awakened One," and he began preaching to others. He preached that in order to free ourselves from suffering, we should understand the **Four Noble Truths**: the truth of suffering, the truth of the cause of suffering, the truth of the extinguishing of suffering, and the truth of the method of extinguishing suffering. To gain this "enlightenment" or "awakening," we should extinguish all desires and **attachments** to this world. We can do this by practicing **meditation**, undergoing

さらに「**八正道**(八つの正しい行い)」について説き、人が四聖諦に至るために実践すべきさまざまなことを示しました。こうした仏陀による根本の教えが、仏教として知られるようになりました。

あらゆるものは永続せず、故に「**空**」であると仏教は教えています。この世への一時的な執着にとどまらず、「**無常**」への深い理解を得ることで人間は真の心の安寧を得ることができる。仏教は**慈悲深く**そう伝えているのです。

■仏教が大きく分裂した際の流派にはどんなものがありますか?

仏教はインドで発生しました。釈迦が悟りに到達して説法を始めた数百年後、仏教はアジアのさまざまな地域へと広がりました。そして広がるにつれ、各地で違うふうに影響を受けていったのです。

東南アジアで広まった仏教は専従の僧を重視したものであり、一般信者は食べ物などの供物を差し出して僧たちを支えました。この流派は**上座部仏教**、あるいはヒナヤナ仏教として知られるようになりました。それはまた専従の僧になった人しか救われないということから、現在は「**小乗仏教**」とも呼ばれています。

別の流派の仏教がヒマラヤ山脈を越えて中国へと伝わり、終には日本まで到達しました。これがマハヤナ仏教として知られるようになり、現

spiritual exercises and following the **precepts**. He then preached the **Eightfold Noble Path**, the varieties of actual practice one can follow to fulfill the Four Noble Truths. These fundamental teachings came to be known as Buddhism.

Buddhism teaches that all things are impermanent and therefore "**empty**." By going beyond momentary attachment to the world and gaining a deep understanding of "**emptiness**," human beings can achieve true peace of mind. This is the **compassionate** message of Buddhism.

◼ What are the main types of Buddhism?

Buddhism began in India. Several centuries after Shakyamuni reached enlightenment and began teaching, Buddhism spread to various parts of Asia. As it spread, it was influenced differently in each area.

In Southeast Asia, Buddhism focused on priests who spent all of their time in religious practices. Ordinary believers supported them with food and offerings. This tradition became known as Theravada or Hinayana Buddhism. It is also called "the **Lesser Vehicle**," because salvation is only possible for the community of priests.

Another tradition of Buddhism traveled over the Himalayas into China, eventually reaching Japan. This tradition became known as Mahayana Buddhism,

在は「**大乗仏教**」とも呼ばれています。この流派は生きるものすべてが仏の本性である「**仏性**」を持ち、仏になることができると考えています。そしてまた自身が**救われる**だけでは充分でない、人は生きるものすべての救いを追求すべきだと教えています。

◾️仏教はどのようにして日本にやって来たのですか?

5世紀ごろにはインドの仏僧が中国へ、中国の仏僧がインドへと赴き始めています。仏教が中国から朝鮮半島に伝わったのは372年のことでした。仏教の正式な日本への伝来については、『**日本書紀**』に記録が残っています。それによると、欽明天皇が538年から552年の間に**仏像**や経典などを朝鮮から受け取ったということです。もちろんそれ以前にも、中国や朝鮮から来た仏教徒たちが日本に**参拝所**を設けていました。

「聖徳太子」(574-622) は仏教を奨励し、仏教寺院の建立に貢献し、経典の**注釈書**を著したことなどで高く評価されています。

◾️奈良時代と平安時代、仏教はどのように受け入れられていたのですか?

仏教が日本に到来すると、最初にそれを朝廷と貴族が取り入れました。僧は一般の人々に教えを説くことを許されていませんでした。

and is also called "the **Greater Vehicle**." This tradition believes all living beings have *bussho*, **buddha nature**, and can become a buddha. It also teaches that gaining **salvation** for oneself is not enough. One should seek salvation for all living beings.

◉ How did Buddhism come to Japan?

Around the 5th century, Indian Buddhist priests began traveling to China, and Chinese priests began traveling to India. Buddhist teachings reached the Korean peninsula from China in 372. The official transmission of Buddhism to Japan is described in the *Nihon Shoki*, the "**Chronicle of Japan**." It says Emperor Kimmei of Japan received an **image of the Buddha** and sutras from the Korean peninsula sometime between 538 and 552. Of course, Buddhists from China and Korea had established **places of worship** in Japan before that, too.

Prince Shotoku, Shotoku Taishi (574–622), is credited with promoting Buddhism, supporting the building of Buddhist temples, and writing **commentaries** on sutras.

◉ How was Buddhism received in Nara and Heian periods?

When Buddhism first arrived in Japan, it was adopted by the imperial court and the nobility. Priests were not allowed to teach the common people.

初期の仏僧とは基本的には役人であり、国から俸禄(ほうろく)をもらい、儀式などを執り行なって国家の平安を祈ることを仕事としていました。当時の日本人は疫病が「**怨霊**」によって引き起こされると信じていたため、これらの僧は怨霊を**鎮める**ための祈禱をするよう政府に要請されていたのです。またその祈禱によって作物を育て、朝廷への**反乱**をなくすことができるとも信じられていました。

　つまり、政府は政府自身を護るために仏教を用いたのであり、そのため仏教に関連するものは僧も寺院も教えもすべて厳しく管理されました。当時の仏教とはすべての国民にとってのものではなく、社会のエリートたちだけのためにあるものだったのです。実際、仏僧は一般の人々と接触を持つことが許されておらず、そのため頻発していた民衆の反乱を僧が率いることは一切ありませんでした。僧が一般の人々に仏教を広め始めるのは後になってからのことです。

■奈良時代と平安時代の間に仏教はどのように変わったのですか？

　仏教が日本に到来した時、都は奈良にありました。その時代、朝廷は現在「**南都**(なんと)**六宗（奈良仏教)**」として知られる六つの宗派を庇護(ひご)しました。この六宗は**学派**というふうに呼ばれていますが、それは学僧たちが一つの宗派に限定することなく複数の宗派の教えを学ぶことができたからで

The first Buddhist priests were basically civil employees. They received salaries from the government. Their occupation was to carry out ceremonies and pray for the safety and peace of the nation. Japanese of that day believed that epidemics were caused by *onryo*, **vengeful spirits**. So these priests were called on to offer Buddhist prayers to **pacify** the spirits that caused epidemics. Their prayers were also believed to make crops grow and stop **uprisings** against the imperial court.

In other words, the government used Buddhism to protect itself, and it strictly controlled Buddhist priests, temples and teachings. Buddhism at this time was not a religion for all the Japanese people. It was only for the elite. In fact, Buddhist priests were not allowed to have contact with the common people. This prevented a priest from becoming a leader of any kind of popular movement that might oppose the government. It was only later that priests began to spread Buddhism among the common people.

◼ How did Buddhism change between the Nara and Heian periods?

When Buddhism arrived in Japan, the capital was at Nara. The imperial court sponsored six different teachings which are now referred to as "the Six Nara Schools of Buddhism." They are called **schools**, because students of Buddhism could focus on several forms of teaching instead of just one. The headquarters for all

す。その中心地とされていたのは東大寺でした。

やがて仏僧たちは朝廷を動かそうとして政治に**干渉し**始めます。そこで朝廷は都を奈良から現在の京都、平安京へと遷都することに決め、寺院には移動を許しませんでした。朝廷は問題のもととなる仏僧たちから逃れることを望んでいました。

新しい都ができあがると、桓武天皇は二人の**敬虔(けいけん)な**僧を見出して京都における仏教の拠点づくりを任せました。その二人とは最澄と空海です。最澄は比叡山に天台宗を、空海は高野山に真言宗を開くことを許されました。この二僧が平安時代の仏教を導いていきます。

■ 仏教は初め、どのようにして死や葬式と結びつくようになったのですか?

神道において死や**死体(けが)**は穢れであり、そのいずれに触れても清めることが必要とされていました。しかし仏教がそのような穢れを除く方法をもたらしました。仏教では、僧がまじないや儀式を行うことで死霊を変身させ、死んだ後でもなお悟りへと導くことが可能でした。そして、生者は死者のために祈ることで最終的に仏になることができました。

仏教と葬式の結びつきは古いものです。早くも685年にはすべての貴族家庭に「**仏壇**」を置くことが義務

of them was at Todaiji.

Buddhist priests began to try to influence the imperial court and **interfere** in politics. So when the imperial court decided to move the capital city from Nara to Heian, present-day Kyoto, it did not allow the temples to move. The court wanted to be free from Buddhist priests who had caused trouble.

Once the new capital was established, Emperor Kammu found two **devout** priests who he trusted to establish Buddhist centers in Kyoto: Saicho and Kukai. Saicho won approval to establish the Tendai sect on Mt. Hiei and Kukai won approval to establish the Shingon sect on Mt. Koya. These two priests led Buddhism in the Heian period.

▶ How did Buddhism first become associated with death and funerals?

In Shinto tradition, death and **corpses** were impurities. Any contact with either required purification. However, Buddhism offered a way to eliminate the impurities that the Japanese associated with death. With incantations and rituals performed by priests, Buddhism was able to transform the spirits of the dead. It could lead these spirits to enlightenment—even after death. If the living prayed for the soul of the deceased, that person could eventually become a Buddha.

The connection between Buddhism and funerals began early. As early as 685, the imperial court ordered that every aristocratic household should have

づけられ、家人は仏壇を使って先祖を礼拝供養することとされました。日本における最初の**火葬**は、ある修行僧（元興寺の道昭）のものでした。それが700年のことであり、やがて火葬は朝廷や貴族たちの間に広まります。その後、火葬や仏壇を用いる慣習は違う階層の人々へと伝わり、どこの家庭でも僧に頼んで死の穢れを除く儀式を執り行なってもらうようになりました。

日本における火葬の割合はほぼ99%です。

▣ 仏教における「来世」とはどのようなものですか?

仏教には「六道」という六つの世界が存在するという考え方があります。人はこの六つの世界で**輪廻転生**をくりかえしているものであり、これを免れる唯一の方法が悟りを得て解脱することだとされています。

悪事を働いた者は地獄の一つに生まれ変わります。地獄を支配しているのは閻魔という恐ろしい審判者であり、一人一人の人生を見直してそれにふさわしい地獄へと送ります。地獄には八大地獄と、十六小地獄があります。悟りを達成した者は**極楽浄土**へと生まれ変わります。

今日の日本人で、来世があると本当に信じている人は、ほとんどいません。

▣ 「末法」とはどんなものですか?

平安時代（794-1185）末期、日本は不安の

a *butsudan*, a **family Buddhist altar**. The families were supposed to use the altar to worship their ancestors. The first **cremation** in Japan was that of a monk. It took place in 700, and before long the practice of cremation spread within the imperial court and the noble families. Later the customs of cremation and family altars spread to other parts of society. Families called on the Buddhist priests to carry out the rituals that removed the impurities that surrounded death.

The cremation rate in Japan is close to 99%.

◼ What is "the afterlife" like in Buddhism?

Buddhism holds that there are Six Realms of Existence (*Rokudo*). A person is **reincarnated** and reborn repeatedly in the cycle of these realms. The only way to escape this cycle is to gain enlightenment.

Those who have done evil are reborn in one of the hells. The ruler of hell is Emma, a frightening judge, who reviews each person's life and sends him to an appropriate hell. There are 8 great hells and 16 lesser hells. Those who have achieved enlightenment are reborn in the **Pure Land of Amida Buddha**.

Few Japanese today actually believe in the afterlife.

◼ What is *mappo*?

In the late Heian period (794–1185) Japanese entered

時代に突入しました。こうなった理由の一つには、仏法に関する三つの時代（三時＝正法→像法→末法）の存在を信じる風潮が強くなったということがあります。これによると最初の時代は仏陀がこの世に降誕した後の1000年間であり、ここでは信者が教えを行うことによって救われました。二番目の1000年間では、経典を理解するとこによって救われました。三番目の1000年間では、救われるためのただ一つの希望が極楽浄土の教えを信仰することでした。

仏教界は、「末法」と呼ばれる三番目の時代が1052年ごろに始まったと見込んでいました。これを背景に、鎌倉仏教の創始者たちは人間が救われるための新しい構想を練り上げていきました。

■ 経典（「お経」）とはどんなものですか？

「お経」とは仏の教えを集めたものです。おそらく今から2000年ほど前に**まとめられた**と考えられ、それは釈迦の入滅からは約400年後に当たります。お経の内容は仏陀による直接の教えではありませんが、その言わんとするところを含んでいます。これが弟子たちを通して**口承**で伝えられました。

「心経（般若心経）」は一般に最も親しまれているお経であり、「妙法蓮華経（法華経）」は日本文化に最大の影響を与えたお経です。仏陀が生者を見守っている、また誰もが仏になることができると妙法蓮華経は伝えています。

a period of anxiety. One possible reason for this was the increase in the belief that there were three periods of the Buddhist dharma or law. According to this, the first period was the first 1,000 years after the Buddha lived on earth. In this period, believers could achieve salvation by way of living teachers. In the second 1,000 years, believers could achieve salvation by understanding the sutras. In the third 1,000 years the only hope for salvation was through faith in the teachings of the Pure Land.

Buddhist scholars estimated that the third period, called *mappo* or "the latter days of the Buddhist law," began in about 1052. Against this background, the creators of Kamakura Buddhism developed new ideas of how humans could achieve salvation.

▣ What are sutras (*okyo*)?

Sutras, *okyo*, are the teachings of Buddha. They were probably **compiled** around 2,000 years ago, which is some four centuries after Shakyamuni entered extinction. Sutras are not the direct teachings of the Buddha, but they contain the essence of his teachings. This was passed down by **oral tradition** through his disciples.

The *Heart Sutra* (*Hannya Shin-gyo*) is one of the most popular. The *Lotus Sutra* (*Hoke-kyo*) is the most influential sutra in Japanese culture. It says that the Buddha watches over and protects the living. It also says that everyone can become a Buddha.

◼ 人はなぜ、お経を毛筆で書き写すのですか?

本来、お経を手で書き写すこと(「**写経**」)は仏教の教えを広めるための一手段でした。しかし、現在では精神修行のようなものとされています。最も一般的なものは般若心経の写経ですが、これは内容が簡潔でわずか262字しかないためです。

◼ 仏像を彫ることはどんな功徳がありますか?

お経を書き写したり**仏像**を彫ったりするのは、できあがったものを奉納するためです。どちらもお寺のため、他者の**救い**のために捧げられます。

仏像は「木に刻み込む」というよりはむしろ「木から彫り出す」と言われています。ある仏教語に「一刀三礼」というものがあり、一刀を入れるごとに三度礼拝します。故に彫り手は信仰を実践する一つの形として仏像を作ります。

数多くの彫像は弘法大師のような仏教界の重鎮の作だとされています。実のところこの中には、彫ったのは彫刻家で、仕上げだけ僧が施したというものもあります。**入魂式**を行う如何にかかわらず、**最後の一彫り**を入れた僧が制作者と言われることになっています。

◼ 禅とは、どんなものですか?

禅は13世紀初頭に日本へと伝わりました。栄

▣ Why do people copy sutras with brush and ink?

Originally, **copying of Buddhist sutras** (*shakyo*) by hand was a way of spreading Buddhist teachings. Now, however, it is regarded as a spiritual practice in itself. The most commonly copied sutra is the *Heart Sutra*, because its message is concise and it is only 262 characters.

▣ What is gained by carving a Buddhist image?

Copying a sutra and carving a **Buddhist image** are both forms of offerings. They both contribute to the temple and to the **salvation** of other people.

Rather than "carving" the image, the sculptor is said to "dig out" the Buddha within the wood. There is a saying that "with one stroke one pays reverence three times." Therefore, the carver makes an image as a form of religious practice.

A number of carved images are attributed to great Buddhist figures like Kobo Daishi. In actual fact, some of these are carved by sculptors and then are given one final finishing touch by a priest. Whether or not it is done at the **consecration ceremony**, the priest who makes the **final stroke** is said to be the sculptor.

▣ What is Zen?

Zen was brought to Japan beginning in the 13th cen-

西と道元によってもたらされ、栄西は臨済宗を、道元は曹洞宗を開きました。この二宗には細い違いがありますが、**座って瞑想すること**が重要だとする点においては軌を一にしています。日本の禅宗は**禁欲的な**鍛錬が重視されますが、これは在家の身にあって、悟りを得た者の指導を仰ぎながら修行を行う人たちも同様です。

▣ 空海とはどんな人物でしたか？

空海（774-835）と最澄（767-822）は初期日本仏教界の二大スターでした。空海は四国で生まれ、京都に上って**儒教、道教、仏教**について学びます。そして最終的に仏門に入りました。

空海は唐で仏教を学ぶ機会を与えられました。三年間、師である恵果のもとで**密教**の修行をし、並外れた才能を表して師から究極の奥義を伝授されます。空海は多くの経典、図画、儀式を執り行うための法具などを持って日本に戻りました。

帰国した空海は日本に真言宗を開き、天皇の後ろ盾を得ます。高野山には金剛峰寺と呼ばれる真言宗の**僧院**を建立することが許され、さらに京都にある東寺という大寺院を**下賜されました**。

空海の死後、天皇は「弘法大師」の諡を授けました。その偉業の数々は記録に残されており、

tury. It was brought by Eisai, who founded the Rinzai sect, and Dogen, who founded the Soto sect. These sects differ in the details, but they agree in stressing the importance of **seated meditation**. Japanese Zen Buddhism stresses **monastic** discipline. This includes living and practicing in a community under the guidance of a teacher who has gained enlightenment.

◼ Who was Kukai?

Kukai (774–835) and the older Saicho (767–822) are the two superstars of early Japanese Buddhism. Kukai was born in Shikoku and went to Kyoto to study **Confucian**, **Taoist** and Buddhist teachings. Eventually he entered the Buddhist priesthood.

He was given the opportunity to study Buddhism in T'ang China. He studied **Esoteric Buddhism** for three years under the master Hui-kuo. Kukai showed exceptional talent, and his master taught him the ultimate Esoteric teachings. Kukai returned to Japan with a great number of sutras, images and implements necessary for carrying out ceremonies.

Upon his return, he founded Shingon or Esoteric Buddhism in Japan and won the support of the emperor. He was given permission to establish a **monastery** for Shingon studies on Mt. Koya called Kongobuji. In addition, he was **entrusted** with the great Toji temple in Kyoto.

When he died, the emperor gave him the **posthumous title** Kobo Daishi, "great teacher who spread the

加えて熱狂的な崇拝者が数多く生まれました。空海の功績には、「仮名」文字の配列（いろは順）を創ったこと、重要な堤防を造ったこと、著名な仏像を彫ったこと、著名な詩を書いたこと、**四国八十八箇所巡礼**の道筋をつけたことがあると考えられています。

■真言宗とは、どんなものですか？

空海が開いた真言宗は「密教」を基盤としており、「密教」とは「秘密の教え」を意味します。真言宗によると、日本に到来した初期の仏教は一般信者が理解できるように簡略化されたものであり、根本仏である大日如来の教えは彼らには容易に理解できるものではないということです。

真言宗の際立っているところは、人は仏と一体になることができると説いていることであり、これは「即身成仏」と呼ばれています。この段階に到達すべく、人は身振りや真言や曼荼羅を用いて仏陀との交信を試みます。胎蔵界曼荼羅と金剛界曼荼羅というものは、両方そろうことによって宇宙全体を視覚的に表現するものです。こうした目や口や身体をつかった手法が、文字で残されたものよりも重要だ考えられていました。

■最澄とはどんな人物でしたか？

最澄（767-822）は奈良で仏僧になりました。しかし、正式な僧として政府のために儀式を行

teachings." In addition to his impressive documented accomplishments, a cult developed around him. He is credited with creating the *kana* syllabary, building important dams, sculpting famous images of Buddha, writing famous poems and originating the **Shikoku pilgrimage of 88 temples**.

◼ What is the Shingon sect?

Founded by Kukai, the Shingon sect is a form of Esoteric Buddhism or *Mikkyo*. The term *mikkyo* refers to "hidden teachings." According to Shingon, the early Buddhism that reached Japan was simplified so that ordinary believers could understand. The Shingon sect says that the true Buddha is Dainichi Nyorai (Maha Vairocana), whose teachings are not easily understood by ordinary believers.

The distinctive teaching of Shingon Buddhism is that a person can become a buddha in his or her own body. This teaching is called *sokushin jobutsu*. To reach this stage, a person uses mudras, mantras and mandalas in order to communicate with the Buddha. The Womb Realm Mandala and the Diamond Realm Mandala together form a visual representation of the entire universe. These visual, verbal and physical methods were considered more important than written scripture.

◼ Who was Saicho?

Saicho (767–822) became a Buddhist priest in Nara. But he became dissatisfied with the priests of the

うだけのような自分の立場に不満を持ち始めます。最澄は奈良を出て京都の北東にある比叡山に庵を結び、そこで修行に励むとともに仏教の真の教えを広めるための方法を学ぶことにしました。

桓武天皇は、都を京都に遷都した際に最澄という名の敬虔な僧のことを知りました。最澄を庇護し、804年には徹底的に仏教を学ばせるために中国へと留学させます。最澄は仏教の経典や書籍などを集め、天台教学を授けられました。帰国後は妙法蓮華経について教え始め、やがて後の天台宗となる教えを学ぶための主要な拠点を設けることが許されます。この拠点は比叡山に築かれました。

◾️ 天台宗とは、どんなものですか？

日本の天台宗は最澄によって806年に開かれたもので、中国の天台宗とは同じ伝統宗派に属しています。天台宗は真言宗とともに、平安時代（794-1185）の日本仏教において圧倒的な勢力を誇った宗派でした。

天台宗は**無常**（あらゆるものは永続せず、とどまることがない）という大乗の教えに基づいています。先に奈良仏教側が、悟りに達することができない衆生が存在すると唱えたことがありました。最澄はこの選民的な考え方とは対照的に、一切の衆生は悟ることができる（衆生済度）と説いています。

temples, who seemed to be concerned only with ceremonies for the government. He left Nara and built a **hut** on Mt. Hiei, northeast of Kyoto, where he could study, practice and learn how to spread the true teachings of Buddhism.

When Emperor Kammu moved the capital to Kyoto, he learned about this devoted priest named Saicho. Kammu supported Saicho and sent him to China in 804 to study Buddhism intensively. Saicho collected Buddhist works and received instruction in T'ien-t'ai teachings. When he returned, he began lecturing on the *Lotus Sutra* and was eventually able to establish a major center for the study of what in Japan came to be called Tendai Buddhism. This center was built on Mt. Hiei.

▣ What is the Tendai sect?

The Tendai sect of Buddhism was founded in 806 by Saicho. It is the Japanese counterpart of the Chinese T'ien-t'ai sect. Together with the Shingon sect, it was a dominant sect of Japanese Buddhism during the Heian period (794–1185).

Tendai is based on the Mahayana teaching of **emptiness**—all things are impermanent and devoid of existence. Prior to Saicho, Nara Buddhism said there is a class of beings who are not capable of attaining enlightenment. In contrast to this elitist view, Saicho taught that *all* sentient beings are capable of enlightenment.

誰もが仏性を持っているという最澄の信条は、あらゆる形式の日本仏教に大きく影響するようになっていきました。最澄はまた、天台僧は他人を救う助けとなることをもって自身が救われる道とすべきだ、大乗の教えに従って生きることで菩薩となるべきだと言っています。

　天台宗は、鎌倉仏教の主な宗祖たちを輩出したことから、重要な存在となっています。

■法然とは、どんな人物でしたか？

　法然（1133-1212）は若い頃、天台宗を学ぶために比叡山へと送られました。しかし、自分が学んだことに対する不満を抱いたままの日々が続きます。法然は自分の力で悟りに到達することができると信じていましたが、思うようにはいきませんでした。後に、ある注釈書と出会い、新しい真理というものを知ります。そこには、凡庸な存在のものは自分で悟りに達する力を持ってはいないということが書かれていました。法然はそのとき、最善の道とは阿弥陀にすがり切ることなのだと納得しました。

　法然は比叡山を出て、ひたすら仏陀の名を唱えるという「専修念仏」を教え始めます。救いを得るためには僧でなくてはならないという考えを棄てて、政府の許しを得ずに自分の思うところを説きました。法然が行なったことは古参の奈良宗派や比叡山の僧たち、そして政府を敵に回すものとなりました。専修念仏を説くこと

His belief that everyone has buddha-nature became highly influential in all forms of Japanese Buddhism. Saicho also said that Tendai priests should help to save others as a way to save themselves. The priests should become bodhisattvas by living according to Mahayana teachings.

The Tendai sect is important because the founders of the major sects of the Kamakura period began their studies on Mt. Hiei.

▣ Who was Honen?

As a young man, Honen (1133–1212) was sent to Mt. Hiei to study Tendai Buddhism, but he remained discontented with what he learned. Honen believed that he could reach enlightenment through his own powers, but he was unsuccessful. Then he found a commentary that taught a new truth. It said that ordinary beings do not have the ability to attain enlightenment on their own. He then understood that the best way was to rely completely on Amida.

Honen left Mt. Hiei and began teaching "the exclusive practice of the *nembutsu*," invoking the name of the Buddha Amida. He gave up the idea that one had to be a priest in order to gain salvation. He preached his message without the permission of the government. Honen's actions challenged the older Nara schools, the Mt. Hiei priests, and the government.

を止めようとしない、その姿勢を脅威と見なされ、法然は流刑にされてしまいます。しかしその教えは庶民の心に強く訴えるものがあり、大きな支持を得たのでした。

■ 浄土宗とは、どんなものですか？

浄土教の一宗派である浄土宗は法然によって開かれました。**西方極楽浄土**へと往生するための念仏（「南無阿弥陀仏」という言い回しであり、「私は阿弥陀仏に帰依します」を意味する）を説いていることで知られています。

浄土宗は阿弥陀を慈悲の仏とし、**長い年月をかけて徳積みをすることで極楽浄土を創った**と見なしています。阿弥陀は48の願を立てており、その中で最も重要なものは、死に際に阿弥陀の名を10回呼べば誰でも極楽往生させるとの約束です。これが阿弥陀からすべての人間へ向けられた慈悲の心です。

■ 親鸞とは、どんな人物でしたか？

法然の**弟子**であった親鸞（1173-1263）もまた、専修念仏を説いたために都を追われました。法然同様、親鸞は後に放免となります。しかし法然の死後、他の弟子たちが自己流に解釈した念仏を説き勧めていることに気付きます。親鸞は師の「真の教え」を伝えることに努め、これが浄土真宗となりました。

They had him banished because they saw his insistence on this "exclusive practice" as a threat. However, his teachings greatly appealed to ordinary people and he drew a significant following.

◼ What is the Jodo Sect?

The Jodo Sect of Pure Land Buddhism was founded by Honen. It is known for preaching the *nembutsu* (the phrase "*Namu Amida Butsu*" which means "I believe in the Buddha Amida") in order to gain rebirth in the **Pure Land in the West**.

The Jodo Sect sees Amida as a Buddha of compassion, who created the Pure Land through the accumulation of merit and power over **aeons**. Amida made a series of 48 **vows**. The most important is the promise of rebirth within his realm to anyone who calls Amida's name ten times at death. This is his compassionate promise to all human beings.

◼ Who was Shinran?

As a **disciple** of Honen, Shinran (1173–1263) was also banished from the capital for preaching the exclusive practice of the *nembutsu*. Like Honen, he was later pardoned. But after Honen's death, Shinran found other Honen disciples preaching their own interpretations of the *nembutsu*. Shinran attempted to preach his teacher's "true teaching," and this became the Jodo Shin Sect, or "true essence of Pure Land Buddhism."

◨浄土真宗とは、どんなものですか？

親鸞は法然にならって、功徳は「**自力**」で身に供えることはできないと唱えました。功徳は阿弥陀の本願力によって得られるものであり、人はその「**他力**」にすべてをゆだねきるべきだというのが親鸞の信条です。浄土真宗は、阿弥陀が救うと願を立てたのだから既に皆救われている、故に皆その感謝を表して念仏を**唱える**だけでいいと教えています。この点が浄土宗との主な違いです。

◨日蓮とは、どんな人物でしたか？

日蓮（1222-1282）は現在の千葉県にある安房地方で生まれました。幼い頃に僧になろうと決め、京へ上って比叡山で学んだ後、もう一度安房へと戻ります。

この遊学によって日蓮は、妙法蓮華経（みょうほうれんげきょう）が唯一の真の教えであると強く思うようになり、他の教えはみな邪法であると見なしました。これが他宗派を激怒させ、日蓮はよそでの布教を強いられます。そして日蓮は「幕府」のある鎌倉に行くことにしました。

自然災害や疫病、飢饉などが次々と起こり、続いてモンゴル皇帝フビライ・カーンの侵略の手がのびてきました。こうした出来事によって日蓮は、妙法蓮華経を信じることのみが救われる道だと確信します。日蓮は「立正安国論」（りっしょうあんこくろん）を政府に提出し、自身の意見を発表しました。そして、その信条が災いして伊豆へ、後に佐渡へと**流さ**

◼ What is the Jodo Shin Sect?

Shinran followed Honen in saying that wisdom is not reached by the **effort of the self**, *jiriki*. He believed that wisdom comes from the powers of Amida's vow. One should trust completely in the powers of Amida Buddha, *tariki*. The main difference with the Jodo Sect is that the Jodo Shin Sect says that we are already saved because Amida vowed to save us. Therefore, we merely **recite** the *nembutsu* as an act of thankfulness.

◼ Who was Nichiren?

Nichiren (1222–82) was born in Awa province, in present-day Chiba prefecture. As a child he decided to become a priest. He went to Kyoto to study at Mt. Hiei, before once again returning to Awa province.

As a result of his studies, he became convinced that the *Lotus Sutra* was the only true teaching. He denied the truth of all other teachings. This made other sects angry and he was forced to carry out his teachings elsewhere. He selected Kamakura, location of the *bakufu*, the military government.

A series of natural disasters, epidemics and famines occurred. They were followed by the threat of invasion of the country by the Mongol leader Kublai Khan. These events convinced Nichiren that the Japanese could only be saved if they embraced the *Lotus Sutra*. Nichiren announced his ideas to the government in *Treatise on the Establishment of the True Dharma and*

れます。

すべての他宗派への非難、攻撃的な行動、自身の信奉者たちの武装などが日蓮に**迫害**をもたらします。しかし、その新旧を**融合**させた仏教には鎌倉武士たちが求めていたものがありました。武士たちは日蓮のことを指導者と見なし、少なからず自軍の大将にも似た存在のように考えていました。

▣ 日蓮宗とは、どんなものですか？

法然と親鸞は念仏することを推奨しました。一方、日蓮が推進したのは「南無妙法蓮華経（私は妙法蓮華経に帰依します）」という「題目」を繰り返し唱えることでした。

▣ 一遍とは、どんな人物でしたか？

一遍（1239-1289）は十歳のときに僧になろうと決めました。比叡山の延暦寺で天台宗の教えを学びますが、それは自分にとって満足のいくものではありませんでした。一遍は九州へと渡り、そこで敬虔な浄土教信者となりました。通説によると、一遍は還俗して妻をめとり、1271年に再び**出家した**ということになっています。

一遍は浄土教に真言宗や神道の民俗的要素を結びつけました。「遊行上人」として知られ始めていた一遍は、救いの道として阿弥陀の名前を唱えること（「南無阿弥陀仏」）の大切さを説き、各地を渡る間に「南無阿弥陀仏決定往生六十万

the Peace of the Nation (Rissho Ankokuron). He was **banished** to Izu and later to Sado for what he believed.

Nichiren's attacks on the other sects, his aggressive behavior and the arming of his followers brought **persecution**. But his **fusion** of old and new Buddhism filled a need among the warriors of Kamakura. They saw him as a master, similar in many ways to their military leaders.

▣ What is the Nichiren Sect?

While Honen and Shinran advocated the *nembutsu*, Nichiren promoted the chanting of the title (*daimoku*) of the name of the *Lotus Sutra:* "*Namu Myoho Renge-kyo*" ("*I believe in the Lotus Sutra*").

▣ Who was Ippen?

Ippen (1239–89), at the age of ten, decided to become a priest. He studied Tendai teachings at Enryakuji on Mt. Hiei. But his studies left him unfulfilled. He traveled to Kyushu where he became a devout Pure Land Buddhist. It is generally thought that Ippen gave up being a priest, took a wife, and then **became a priest** again in 1271.

Ippen combined Pure Land teachings with Shingon and folk elements of Shinto. Becoming known as a "wayfaring saint" (*yugyo shonin*), Ippen preached the importance of reciting Amida's name (*Namu Amida Butsu*) as the path to salvation. During his travels,

人」と書かれたお札を配りました。

一遍の独特さは「踊念仏」による布教を行なったことにあり、それは広く大衆に支持されました。親鸞とは対照的に、一切を捨て我を忘れて阿弥陀の名前を唱えさえすればよいと一遍は強調しており、阿弥陀の救いに完全にすがることをその信条としています。一遍は浄土教の一宗派である時宗を開きました。

◼ 栄西とは、どんな人物でしたか？

栄西（1141-1215）は七歳で仏教を学び始めました。延暦寺で天台僧となりましたが、比叡山の僧たちの堕落ぶりに嫌気がさし始めます。栄西は1168年に中国を訪れ、天台宗の僧院を訪れて経典を集めました。1187年には再び中国へと渡り、瞑想と「公案」と密教の要素を組み合わせた臨済宗の師の下で禅を学びました。

「公案」とは理屈では解らないような問いのことであり、禅僧が悟りを理屈抜きに直感することの助けとなります。

1191年、栄西は帰国します。九州と京都で禅を教え、このことが天台宗の僧たちを激怒させました。栄西は『興禅護国論』の中で、禅は天台宗に新しい活力を与え、国家の安泰と繁栄に貢献するものだと主張しています。それでも天台宗側の攻撃は止みませんでした。

he handed out pieces of paper that read: "Believe in Amida Buddha. Definite rebirth. Six hundred thousand believers."

His uniqueness lies in his preaching the "dancing *nembutsu*," ecstatic dancing and preaching that won him a popular following. In contrast with Shinran, Ippen stressed the ecstatic incantation of Amida's name with complete abandonment. He believed in relying totally on the Buddha for salvation. Ippen founded the Ji Sect of Pure Land Buddhism.

◘ Who was Eisai?

Eisai (1141–1215) began studying Buddhist teachings at the age of seven. He became a Tendai monk at Enryakuji, but he became disillusioned by the **loose way of life** on Mt. Hiei. He traveled to China in 1168, and visited Tendai (T'ien-t'ai) monasteries and collected Tendai sutras. In 1187 he traveled to China a second time. He studied Zen under a Rinzai master who combined meditation, *koan* study and esoteric practices.

The *koan* are problems that seem illogical. They help the priest realize enlightenment **intuitively**—not by using logic.

Eisai returned to Japan in 1191. He taught Zen teachings in Kyushu and Kyoto, and this angered Tendai monks. In *The Propagation of Zen for the Protection of the Nation (Kozen gokoku-ron)*, he argued that Zen practice would give new energy to Tendai teachings and contribute to the security and welfare of

栄西は1198年に京都を去って鎌倉に行きました。そして、勢力拡大のために新しい文化を探していた鎌倉幕府の庇護を受けます。栄西は重く用いられ、1202年には建仁寺を建立して同寺の**住職**となり、そこで密教、天台宗、禅の教えを授けました。

◾道元とは、どんな人物でしたか？

道元（1200-1253）は比叡山で天台宗を、栄西の弟子である明全の下で臨済宗を学びました。1223年に中国へと渡り、そこで曹洞宗の長翁如浄禅師の弟子となります。二ヵ月のうちに道元は悟りに至り、師から曹洞宗の**継承者**として認められました。

1227年に帰国すると、道元はひたすら座禅に打ち込むことを**唱道**します。そして都の天台僧たちの不興を買い、やがて**大著**『正法眼蔵』の執筆に取りかかりました。その中に道元は、すべての人が仏になる力を秘めていると書いています。蓮華座でひたすら瞑想すれば誰もが悟り得ると述べており、これを「**只管打坐**」と呼びました。道元は禅の教化を行うために朝廷から承認を得ようしましたが、天台宗側からの弾圧で自分のいる寺を追われることとなりました。

the nation. This did not stop the attacks of the Tendai establishment.

He left Kyoto in 1198 and went to Kamakura. He received support from the Kamakura shogunate, which was looking for new cultural elements to strengthen its powers. He was welcomed and in 1202 was made founder and **abbot** of the Kenninji monastery, where he taught esoteric Buddhism, Tendai teachings and Zen.

▣ Who was Dogen?

Dogen (1200–53) studied Tendai teachings on Mt. Hiei and Rinzai teachings under Eisai's disciple Myozen. He traveled to China in 1223. There he studied under the master of the Chan (Soto Zen) school, Chang-weng Ju-ching. Within two months, Dogen achieved enlightenment and was recognized by his master as the **successor** to the tradition of Soto Zen.

Returning to Japan in 1227, he **advocated** single-minded devotion to Zen and thereby provoked the Tendai monks of the capital city. He then began writing his **masterpiece** *Treasury of the True Dharma Eye (Shobogenzo)*. In it he wrote that all people possess the potential to become a Buddha. He said that enlightenment is possible for anyone, if they just **meditate in the lotus position**. He called this *shikan taza*. He tried to get approval from the imperial court to teach Zen. But the Tendai leaders chased him from his temple.

道元は京都からも比叡山からも遠く離れた山地に僧院を建立します。その場所として選んだのは越前（現在の福井県）で、そこに曹洞僧たちに修行を積ませるための道場を設けることとしました。永平寺というこの寺院は今も変わらず禅修行の本場となっており、戒律が厳しいことで知られています。

▣鈴木大拙とは、どんな人物でしたか？

西洋ではダイセツ・T・スズキ（1870–1966）として知られるこの哲人は、その地に禅を伝えることにおいて大変重要な存在でした。その他禅に関する仕事で特筆すべきことは『禅と日本文化』（1938年）の執筆であり、この著作は英語圏の人々に大きな影響を与えました。

▣仏尊には、主にどんな種類のものがありますか？

仏堂や曼荼羅の中では、一つだけでなくいくつもの仏像を目にすることが多いものです。たいていの場合は、中心となる一体を囲んで他種の仏像から成るグループがいくつも配置されています。仏尊には基本的な種類が四つあります。

如来（仏）は**階層**の最上位に位置します。上から順に、最もなじみの深い阿弥陀（光の仏）、薬師（病を治す仏）、大日（宇宙仏）、毘盧舎那、釈迦（前身が釈迦であった仏）と言います。薬師如来は、たいてい周りを小さな如来像によって囲まれていることか

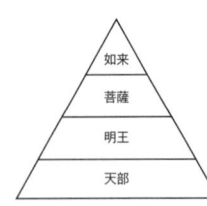

He established a monastery in the mountains far away from Kyoto and Mt. Hiei priests. Dogen selected Echizen (present-day Fukui prefecture) as the site for a temple to train Soto sect monks. This temple, Eiheiji, continues to be a major Zen training institution known for its rigorous discipline.

◼ Who was Daisetsu Suzuki?

Known in the West as Daisetz T. Suzuki (1870–1966), this philosopher was very important in teaching the West about Zen Buddhism. Among other important works on Zen, his *Zen Buddhism and Its Influence on Japanese Culture* (1938) had a major impact in the English-speaking world.

◼ What are the main kinds of Buddhist deities?

In the worship hall of a temple and in mandalas, there is often more than one image. In many cases, a central image is surrounded by groups of other types of images. There are four basic kinds of Buddhist deities.

Nyorai (Buddha, Tathagata) are at the top of the **hierarchy**. In descending order, the most popular are Amida (the Buddha of Light), Yakushi (the Buddha of healing), Dainichi (the great sun Buddha, the cosmic Buddha), Birushana (Vairocana) and Shaka (the historical Buddha). You can recognize Yakushi Nyorai because he is usually surrounded by small Nyorai images. The

ら、それとわかります。東大寺の大仏は毘盧舎那、鎌倉の大仏は阿弥陀です。

これらの仏はたいてい修行僧が着ているような質素な衣をまとい、頭は**剃髪**され、装飾品は付けていません。如来は身体を使って独特の意味を表す姿勢を取り、両手を使って象徴的なポーズ（「印相」）を作っている場合があります。

菩薩は上位から二番目のグループに位置します。これらはいずれ仏となる、霊的に高い位に達した存在です。菩薩は他の人々を助けて悟りの境地へと導いてしまうまで仏となることを「留め置かれて」いる状態にあります。だからこそ慈悲深いと見なされ、信者に愛されているのです。このグループには観音、地蔵、文殊、弥勒などが含まれます。弥勒は次の仏陀となることが決まっていますが、これは当分先の話です。釈迦の悟りから56億7000万年経つまでその日は来ません。およそ2600年前に仏陀が悟ったので、弥勒は長い間待つことになります。

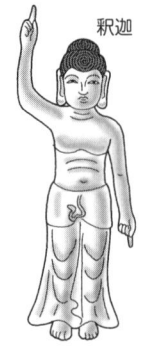

これらの菩薩には、すべての人間への慈悲を表す優しげな表情を浮かべているものが非常に多く見られます。たいていは長髪で、手や首や耳に装飾品をつけており、また手にはさまざまな道具を持っています。

明王は上から三番目に位置します。明王とは明（仏の知恵）を身に付けた者たちの王で、もとはヒンドゥー教の神であり、大日如来の化身として密教に取り入れられました。明王は真言の力によって仏教に**帰依していない者**たちを救

Great Buddha at Todaiji in Nara is Birushana and the Great Buddha at Kamakura is Amida.

These Buddhas usually wear plain clothing like a monk would wear, have a **shaved head**, and wear no accessories. They may have particular symbolic marks on their bodies and be making a symbolic mudra (*inzo*) with their hands.

Bosatsu (Bodhisattva) are the second group from the top. These are beings of great spiritual achievement who will one day become a Buddha. They have "postponed" becoming a Buddha until they have helped others reach Buddhahood. That is why they are seen as compassionate and why they are very popular among believers. This group includes Kannon, Jizo, Monju and Miroku. Miroku is designated to be the next Buddha, but this will not be anytime soon. This will not occur until 5,670,000,000 years after the Shakyamuni's enlightenment. Because the Buddha was enlightened about 2,600 years ago, Miroku still has a long time to wait.

These bodhisattvas very often have a gentle expression showing their compassion for all human beings. They often have long hair; wear bracelets, necklaces, and earrings; and hold various items in their hands.

Myoo are the third from the top. They are kings of wisdom and light and were originally Hindu deities. They were adopted into Esoteric Buddhism as incarnations of the cosmic Buddha. They save **nonbelievers** with the power of sacred words. The most common

います。このグループの中で最も身近なものが不動明王であり、千葉県にある新勝寺（成田山）が信仰の拠点とされています。

明王には、髪を逆立て、恐ろしい顔で、武器を持って、炎に囲まれている姿のものがよく見られます。

天部はこの階層の最下位に位置しています。天部は天上界に住む存在であり、このグループにはヒンドゥー教から取り入れられた別の神々が含まれています。それぞれが固有の力を持ち、中には土着の宗教において非人間的な姿になった天部もあります。最もなじみのあるものは、対となっている梵天と帝釈天（東大寺や東寺に展示）、仁王、もしくは金剛力士（東大寺に展示）、四天王（法隆寺や東寺に展示）、女性尊の弁才天（弁天）、もしくは吉祥天、十二神将、そして大黒天などです。

明王

天部にもまた、恐ろしい姿をしている場合があります。

五番目のグループに含まれる「羅漢（阿羅漢）」たちは、位の高い仏教徒です。寺院によっ

in this group is Fudo Myoo, whose cult is centered at Shinshoji (Narita-san) in Chiba prefecture.

They often have flaming hair, look fierce, bear weapons, and are surrounded by flames.

Tembu are the bottom of the pyramid. They are heavenly beings or deva. This group includes other deities adopted from Hindu. Each has its own powers and some have become objects of local cults. The most popular of this group are the pair Bonten and Taishakuten (seen at Todaiji and Toji); Nio or Kongo-rikishi (seen at Todaiji); the Shitenno or "Four Heavenly Kings" (seen at Horyuji and Toji); the feminine deities Benzaiten, Benten or Kisshoten; the Juni Shinsho or "Twelve Heavenly Generals"; and Daikokuten.

天部

All these deities may have fierce features.

A fifth group includes *rakan* (arhats), who are Buddhists of high spiritual attainment. Certain temples

ては「五百羅漢」と呼ばれる500体の羅漢像を所蔵しているところがあり、それらの像はどこか独特で、面白げな表情をしています。またこのグループにはさまざまな高僧や仏教界の有識者、各宗派の**始祖**といった人たちも入っています。

羅漢

▣像の仏が踏みつけている奇妙な生き物は何ものですか?

いくつかの彫刻には、仏が鬼らしきものに片足をのせている姿が見られます。これらは「邪鬼」という邪神、もしくは怨霊です。邪鬼は懲らしめられているように見えますが、実はすでに**祓い清められて**います。邪鬼が**踏み台**として喜んでその身を差し出しているので、仏は地に触れる必要がありません。邪鬼はまた、特に天部の一つを支えているものを指して「天邪鬼」とも呼ぶこともあります。

▣仏陀はなぜ巻き毛で大きな耳をしているのですか?

仏像の頭にあるらせん状の巻き毛は「螺髪」と呼ばれています。螺髪は悟りを象徴するものです。

耳飾りをつけた像は菩薩であって、仏ではありません。仏陀は悟りを得た時に、耳に穴を残したまま耳飾りを外しています。極端に大きな耳は信者たちの祈りすべてに耳を傾ける準備がで

have statues of 500 arhats, called *gohyaku rakan*. They tend to have unique, somewhat comical expressions. Also in this group are various eminent priests, scholars of Buddhism and **patriarchs** of various schools and sects.

邪鬼

◼ Who are the strange creatures that statues of Buddha step on?

Some sculptures show Buddha with one foot on what looks like a demon. These *jaki* are devils or evil spirits. It seems as though they are being punished. But actually they have been **exorcised**. Out of gratitude, they are offering themselves as a **pedestal**, so the Buddha does not have to touch the ground. They are also called *amanojaku*, especially when they support one of the *Tembu*.

◼ Why does the Buddha have curly hair and big ears?

The spiral curls on the head of statues of the Buddha are called *rahotsu* or *rahatsu*. It is a symbol of enlightenment.

Statues with earrings are bodhisattvas, not buddhas. When Buddha gained enlightenment, he took off his earrings, leaving holes in his ears. The exceptionally large ears are a symbol of his preparation to hear the

白毫 Byakugo
螺髪 Rahotsu

きていることを象徴するものです。

■仏像の眉間には、なぜほくろのようなものがあるのですか？

ほくろのように見えますが、これは「白毫」と呼ばれる白く長い一本の髪の毛を描いたものです。白毫は仏陀が持つと考えられている三十二の身体的特徴の一つであり、多くの像では貴重な石などで表現されています。

■不動明王とは、どういうものですか？

不動明王が象徴しているものは、人間の心掛け次第で向けられる容赦のない厳しさと、同時に持ち合わせた慈悲に溢れる心です。その恐ろしい表情は仏法に敵対するものを強く憎む気持ちを表しています。左目が半眼で右目を見開いているものもあれば、片方は見上げもう片方は見下ろしているものもあります。眉間には第三の目を持つものが多く、口からは**牙**を剥き出しています。片方の手に持った剣は暴力でなく慈悲の心を象徴するものであり、もう片方の手に持った**投げ縄**は煩悩を絡め取るためのものです。日本では不動明王に交通安全のご利益があると考えられており、炎に囲まれた恐ろしげな不動明王のステッカーを買って車のお守りとする人もいます。

prayers of all believers.

◼ Why do Buddhist statues have a mole in the middle of the brow?

It looks like a mole, but this is called *byakugo* and it represents a curl of long white hair. It is one of the 32 physical features that Buddha is thought to possess. In many statues it is represented by a precious stone.

◼ What is Fudo Myoo?

Fudo Myoo, the Immovable King, symbolizes the necessity of being stern with some types of people, but also being compassionate. His fierce expression symbolizes his strong hostility to the enemies of Buddha's truth. His left eye is half-open; his right eye is staring. One eye looks up; the other looks down. Often he has a third eye in the middle of his forehead. **Fangs** stick out of his mouth. In one hand he has a sword, symbolizing compassion not violence. In the other, he has a **lasso**, to entangle passions. In Japan, he is said to ensure safety on the highway. Some Japanese purchase stickers of the frightening figure surrounded with flames as protection for their automobiles.

不動明王

◨ なぜ地蔵は、それほど人に好まれるのですか?

菩薩は仏ではありませんが、仏になる力をすべて持ち合わせています。地蔵は仏になることをせず、人々を助けるために人間界にとどまることを誓いました。このため、地蔵は日本において平安時代から親しまれ、特に一般の人たちの間で好まれてきました。

地蔵はたいてい左手に珠を持ち、右手で杖をついた修行僧の姿で描かれます。旅人や子供の守護者と見なされており、その人たちが天国にたどりつけるよう「三途の川」を渡る手助けをします。「水子供養」の際には、「水子」の加護を地蔵に祈願する例がよく見られます。

◨ なぜ観音は、それほど人に好まれるのですか?

地蔵と同じく観音もまた菩薩です。観音は危機に瀕した人類を包む無限の慈悲を持っており、今生においては人々を護り、死後は信者が極楽浄土へと移る手助けをします。

観音はもともと男性でしたが、安産の守護者として女性の姿が好まれるようになりました。

観音が表すさまざまな姿には、「馬頭観

◼ Why is Jizo so popular?

Bodhisattva, *bosatsu*, are not buddhas, but they have the full power to become buddhas. Jizo pledged not to become a Buddha, but instead to remain in the human world to help people. Because of this, he has been popular in Japan since the Heian period, especially among the common people.

Jizo is usually shown as a monk, holding a jewel in the left hand and a staff in the right hand. He is regarded as the protector of travelers and children and helps them cross *Sanzu no kawa*, similar to the River Styx, in order to reach Paradise. Memorial services for miscarried or aborted fetuses (*mizuko kuyo*) often invoke Jizo, asking for protection of the *mizuko*, literally "water child."

◼ Why is Kannon so popular?

Like Jizo, Kannon is also a bodhisattva (*bosatsu*). Kannon has unlimited compassion for people in danger, protects people in this life and helps transport believers after death to the Pure Land.

Kannon was originally male, but in female form became popular as a protector of women giving birth.

Various representations of Kannon include the

音」、「十一面観音」、「白衣観音」、「千手観音」などがあります。いわゆる「1000の手を持つ観音」には実際のところ16から42の手がついており、これによって観音の無限の慈悲を象徴しています。それぞれの手が25の世界を救うものであり、つまり40の手で1000の世界を救うことを表しています。

阿修羅

■「阿修羅」とはどんなものですか?

もともとヒンドゥー教の神だった「阿修羅」は、実は魔神であり、勇敢な戦士として知られていました。日本仏教において、阿修羅は闘志を燃やして仏法を護ります。興福寺には、六本の腕をもった有名な阿修羅像が所蔵されています。

■「だるま」とは、どんなものですか?

「だるま」は頭と体だけの丸い人形で、目の部分に二つの大きな空白があります。この人形は中国禅の開祖となったインドの僧、達磨大師の姿を表現したものです。達磨は洞窟の中で九年間瞑想し、両腕と両足が不自由になってしまったと言われています。達磨の丸い人形は突いて倒すと、ひとりでに転がって起き上がるようにできています。これは困難から立ち上がる力を象徴しており、故にだるまは**縁起物**と考えられています。

達磨大師像(群馬県)

Horse-headed (*Bato*) Kannon, the Eleven-headed (*Juichi-men*) Kannon, the White-robed (*Byakue*) Kannon, and the Thousand-armed (*Senju*) Kannon. The so-called "Thousand-armed Kannon" actually have between 16 and 42 arms, symbolizing Kannon's infinite compassion. Each arm symbolizes the salvation of 25 worlds, so 40 arms represents the salvation of 1,000 worlds.

▣ What is an *asura*?

Ashura (*Asura*), originally Hindu gods, were actually demon-gods or avatars. They were known as courageous fighters. In Japanese Buddhism, the *asura* use their fierce fighting spirit to protect Buddhism. Kofukuji has a famous statue of an *asura* with six arms.

▣ What is a *daruma*?

A *daruma* is a figure with rounded head and body, with two large spaces for eyes. These figures represent Bodhidharma, the Indian priest who founded Zen Buddhism in China. It is said he spent nine years meditating in a cave and lost the use of his arms and legs. The round figures of Bodhidharma are weighted so that when you tip one over, it will roll upright on its own. This symbolizes the ability to recover from difficulties, so *daruma* are considered **good luck charms**.

だるま人形は、たいてい紙を貼り合わせて赤く色を塗って作られています。願いごとを叶えるための縁起物とされ、特に選挙の当選祈願や作物の豊作祈願などに使用されています。通常、購入時には目が描かれておらず、**願いごと**をする時に自分で片方の目を描き入れ、家の神棚に安置します。そして願いごとが叶った時、もう片方の目を入れます。

　3月の3日と4日には、三鷹市（東京）にある深大寺でだるま市が開かれます。

◾️「大仏」については、どんなことが知られていますか？

　「大仏」とは5メートルぐらいの高さの仏像です。日本には有名な大仏が二つあります。鎌倉大仏は13世紀中ごろから存在しているものであり、像高は約11.4メートルです。かつては寺院の建物の中にありましたが、その建物は1495年に消失してしまいました。それ以来、屋外に安置されています。奈良大仏とは東大寺盧舎那仏像のことで、像高が約15メートルあります。最初に大仏が完成したのは752年のことで、当時は日本一美しい大仏と言われていました。現在の大仏は何度かの再建を経たものです。

東大寺盧舎那仏（奈良県）

◾️お寺とは、どんな造りになっていますか？

　日本で「寺」または「寺院」と呼ばれる仏教施設は僧や**尼僧**が日常生活を送り、儀式などが

Daruma figures are usually made of papier-mache and painted red. They are used as charms for fulfilling a wish, especially success in a public election or a successful harvest. Usually the eyes are not painted in when you buy it. You paint in one eye when you make your **wish**, then put it in the family shrine. When the wish is fulfilled, you paint in the other eye.

On March 3rd and 4th, a market selling *daruma* figures is held at Jindaiji in Mitaka (Tokyo).

◼ What makes a statue a *daibutsu*?

A *daibutsu*, "great Buddha," is about 5 meters or 16 feet tall. There are two famous "great Buddha" statues in Japan. The Kamakura Daibutsu dates from the mid-13th century. It is 11.4 meters (37.4 feet) tall. It was once inside a temple building, but that building was lost in 1495 to flood and earthquake. Since then, it has been out in the open. The Nara Daibutsu is an image of Buddha Vairocana at Todaiji. It is 15 meters (49.2 feet) high. The original was completed in 752, and it was considered the most splendid Buddhist statue in Japan. The current image has been restored several times.

◼ What defines a temple?

Called *tera* or *jiin* in Japanese, Buddhist temples are places where priests or **nuns** usually live and ceremonies

行われる場所です。入り口には、たいてい**瓦屋根**がついた木造の門があります。

境内には通常、「塔」、「本堂」、「講堂」、「鐘楼」、「経蔵」などがあり、住み込みの僧や尼僧がいる場合は「僧坊」や「食堂（じきどう）」もあります。本堂にはたいてい一体から数体の仏像が安置されており、本尊（ほんぞん）の周りに異なる種類の仏像が配置されていることもあります。

明治時代、仏教と神道は公式に分離されました。しかし、時々お寺の敷地内に神社を見かけることがあります。神道の神々が仏たちを護っているところも目にするかもしれません。

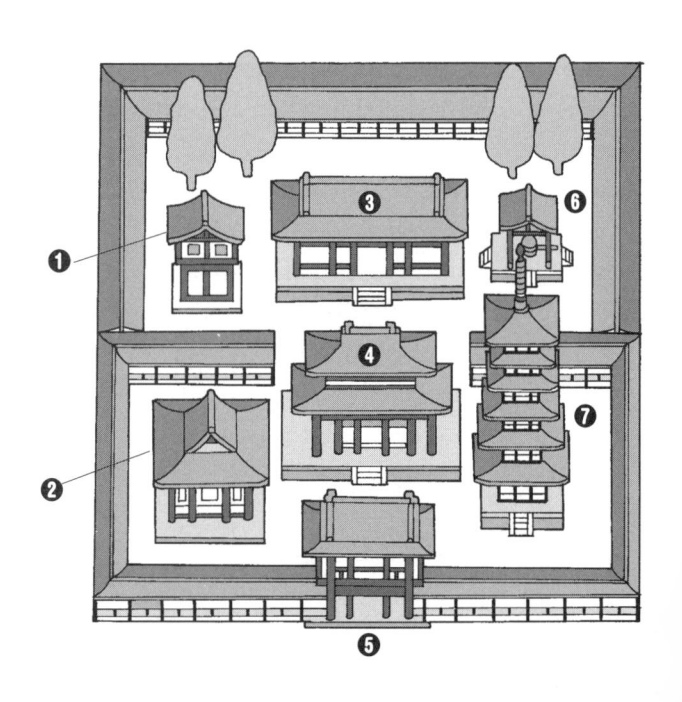

take place. At the entrance to a temple there is usually a wooden gate with a **tile roof**.

The grounds of a temple usually contain a pagoda (*to*), a main hall (*kondo, hondo*), lecture hall (*kodo*), a bell tower (*shoro, shuro*), and a sutra repository (*kyozo*). If there are resident priests or nuns, there is also a dormitory (*sobo*) and dining hall (*jikido*). The main hall usually has one or more images of Buddha. There may be other deities surrounding the main images.

Although Buddhism and Shintoism were officially separated during the Meiji period, you will sometimes see a shrine on the grounds of a temple. You may also see Shinto deities protecting the Buddhas.

境内伽藍
Temple Compound

①僧坊	dormitory
②経蔵	sutra repository
③講堂	lecture hall
④金堂（本堂）	main hall
⑤山門（三門）	gate
⑥鐘楼	bell tower
⑦塔	pagoda

◼ 仏塔とは、どんなものですか？

　仏塔（「塔」）は仏舎利（遺骨）を納めるために建てられます。日本の仏塔は古代インドのストゥーパ(仏舎利塔)に由来しています。ストゥーパはインド仏教の僧院にある大きな建造物でした。すべてが五階建ての仏塔（「五重塔」）ではありませんが、奇数の階数であることが好まれます。

　日本の仏塔は、一本の「心柱」を四本の「側柱」で囲って建てられています。屋根は反り上がっており、大きさが上の階にいくほど小さくなります。屋根の端には通常、「風鐸」がついています。天辺にある「相輪」は、いくつかの「宝輪」があって、その上に「水煙」、「竜車」、一番上が「宝珠」という作りになっています。

　日本の仏塔の中には本物の仏舎利を持たないものもあり、代わりにそれらには経典や法具などが納められています。浅草寺の仏塔には、スリランカから招来した本物の仏舎利が安置されています。

◼ 日本に、お寺はいくつあるのですか？

　日本には約7万7000寺のお寺があります。

◼ なぜお寺の正面には一対の狛犬がいるのですか？

　神社とお寺の正面には、どちらにも一対の「狛犬」が見られます。狛犬は守護する者としての

◾ What is a pagoda?

Pagodas (*to*) are built to store **relics of the Buddha**. The Japanese pagoda derives from the ancient Indian stupa. The stupa was a major structure in the monasteries of Indian Buddhism. Not all are the commonly seen **five-story pagodas** (*goju-no-to*), but odd numbers of stories are definitely preferred.

They are constructed with a central pillar (*shimbashira*) surrounded by four inner pillars (*gawabashira*). The roofs curve upward and grow smaller as they move toward the top. The ends of the roofs usually have **wind-bells** (*futaku*). The finial (*sorin*) on the top has sacred rings (*horin*), topped by a "water flame" ornament (*suien*), a "dragon wheel" ornament (*ryusha*), and a "sacred jewel" ornament (*hoju*) at the very top.

Some pagodas in Japan do not have actual relics of the historical Buddha. Instead they have sutras or sacred ritual implements. The pagoda at Senso-ji has actual relics received from a temple in Sri Lanka.

◾ How many temples are there in Japan?

There are about 77,000 Buddhist temples in Japan.

◾ Why is there a pair of lions in front of a temple?

A pair of "lion dogs" (*koma-inu*) can be found in front of both shrines and temples. They are protective

象徴であり、おそらくは朝鮮、果ては中国から伝来したものです。

■お寺の門のところに立っている、恐ろしい二人組の「仁王」とはどんなものですか？

仁王はもともとヒンドゥー教の神であり、邪悪なものに立ち向かう守護者として仏教に取り入れられました。一方は口を開いて「阿あ！」と言っています。これはサンスクリット・アルファベットの最初の音おんであり、宇宙の始まりを表したものです。もう一方は口を閉じて「吽うん！」。こちらは同じく最後の音に当たるもので、宇宙の終わりを意味します。そのようなことから、前者が阿形、後者が吽形と呼ばれています。仁王たちがお寺の門に立っているのは、悪霊を退け、境内に盗人や鬼が入らないようにするためです。浅草（東京）の浅草寺では、みごとな仁王像を目にすることができます。

ついでですが、お寺の門をくぐる際には「**敷居**」は踏まずに、またぐようにして下さい。

■「地獄絵図」が意図するものとは何ですか？

「地獄絵図」とは悪人たちが地獄で味わうことになる苦しみを描いた絵であり、平面状と巻物状の両方の形式があります。罪人つみびとたちがあの世で向かい合う恐怖を見せることによって、そんな人間を改心させたいという僧たちの願いがこもっています。

symbols, probably introduced from Korea or even China.

◼ What are the pair of fierce *Nio* in temple gates?

The *Nio*, Benevolent Kings, were originally Hindu gods. They were adopted by Buddhists as protectors against evil. One has his mouth open, saying "A!", the first sound of the Sanskrit alphabet, which symbolizes the beginning of the universe. The other has his mouth closed, saying "Un!", from "Hum!" the last sound of the Sanskrit alphabet, which symbolizes the end of the universe. Therefore, the first is called Agyo and the second is called Ungyo. They stand at the gate of a temple to ward off evil spirits and keep the temple grounds free of thieves and demons. You will notice great examples of Nio at Sensoji at Asakusa (Tokyo).

Incidentally, when you go through the gate, step over—not on—the **threshold** (*shikii*).

◼ What is the purpose of a "hell screen" (*jigoku-ezu*)?

"Hell screens," *jigoku-ezu*, are paintings of the sufferings that evil people will endure in hell. These pictures take the form of both scrolls and screens. By showing the horror that sinners faced in the next world, priests hoped to make them change their ways.

「八熱地獄」では、人間でない顔をした鬼たちがさまざまな方法で人間たちに責め苦を与えます。あるものは罪人を金棒で叩き、あるものは罪人を切り刻み、あるものは灼熱の溶けた鉄を罪人ののどに流し込み、あるものは罪人を火あぶりにします。

◼ なぜ仏像には卍(「万字」)の印があるのですか？

「卍」は「すべてがうまくいっている」という意味のサンスクリット語に由来します。日本でこの記号は「万字」と呼ばれ、仏教寺院を表す地図記号としても使用されています。仏教においては吉祥の印であり、仏陀の足跡および仏陀の心を象徴します。また、卍は朝鮮やチベットの仏教にも使用例が見られます。

◼ 現在、日本仏教の主な僧院はどこにあるのですか？

788年、最澄和尚は京都の北西に位置する比叡山に仏教を学ぶための重要な拠点を開きました。この山は延暦寺を中心に天台宗の修行の本場となり、それは他宗派にとっても同様でした。平安仏教を代表する多くの人物たちが、ここで学んでは巣立っていきました。

真言宗（密教）の中心となる僧院は空海によって開かれたものであり、大阪南方にある和歌山県の高野山に位置します。高野山にはユネスコの**世界遺産**に含まれる場所もあり、100寺を超

In the eight "hot hells," demons with non-human heads torture humans in various ways. Some beat sinners with iron clubs. Some slice humans to shreds. Some pour hot metal down the sinner's throat. Some roast sinners in a fire.

◼ Why is there a swastika (*manji*) in Buddhist images?

The word "swastika" comes from the Sanskrit word "svastika" meaning "all is well." In Japanese the symbol is called *manji*. It is sometimes used as a symbol for Buddhist temples on maps. In Buddhism the swastika is auspicious and a sign of good fortune. It symbolizes the Buddha's footprints and the Buddha's heart. It is also found in the Buddhism of Korea and Tibet.

◼ Where are the main Buddhist monasteries today?

The priest Saicho founded an important center for Buddhist studies on Mt. Hiei, northeast of Kyoto, in 788. Centered on Enryakuji temple, this mountain became a center for the Tendai sect and other sects as well. Many of the figures of Heian Buddhism studied here at one time or another.

The main monastery of the Shingon (Esoteric) sect founded by Kukai is on Mt. Koya, south of Osaka in Wakayama prefecture. It is part of a UNESCO **World Heritage** Site and has over 100 temples and

延暦寺(京都府)

える寺院や僧院が集まっています。

　福井県にある永平寺は道元によって1243年に開かれたものであり、修行僧たちを鍛え曹洞宗の伝統を教え込む道場となっています。永平寺は京の都や鎌倉幕府の関心事である俗世的な問題に係わることを嫌って、わざわざその山地に建立されました。今でもそこは戒律の厳しい禅の修行で知られています。

■「駆け込み寺」とはどんなものですか?

　むかし男性が妻を離縁するのは容易いことでしたが、女性が夫と別れるのは難しいものでした。19世紀まで、尼寺の中には夫から逃れようとしている女性を匿ってくれるところがあり、女性はその中のどれかで二年間奉公すれば、夫と離婚することが許されることになっていました。鎌倉の東慶寺はこうした寺の中で最も知られているものの一つです。これらは「駆け込み寺」、または「縁切り寺」と呼ばれていました。

永平寺(福井県)

monasteries.

Eiheiji in Fukui prefecture was founded by Dogen in 1243. It trains monks in the Soto sect Zen tradition. It was purposely built in the mountains away from secular concerns of either the old capital, Kyoto, or the military government at Kamakura. Eiheiji remains known for rigorous Zen monastic training.

◼ What are "refuge temples" (*kakekomidera*)?

In the ancient past, it was easy for a man to divorce his wife, but it was difficult for a woman to divorce her husband. Until the 19th century, some convent temples gave refuge to women who were fleeing from their husbands. If a woman served in one of these temples for two years, she would be allowed to divorce her husband. Tokeiji in Kamakura was one of the best known of these temples. These were called *kakekomidera* ("temples to run to for refuge") or *enkiridera* ("divorce temples").

Buddhism ● 203 ●

■なぜ僧は剃髪(ていはつ)するのですか？

一説によると仏陀が出家する時、髪を切り落として真理を追究すると誓ったと言われています。これが本当か否かは定かではありませんが、仏僧は自己を**飾るもの一切を捨て去る**ため、自身を他宗教の信者から区別するために剃髪します。

■「袈裟(けさ)」が象徴するものとはなんですか？

初期の仏僧はあらゆるものへの執着を**放棄するもの**とされ、着ている衣でさえその辺にあったぼろ布で作ったものでした。中国と日本においてこの衣が儀式などで用いられるようになり、より色鮮やかで豪華なものへと変わっていきました。日本の僧が着ている「袈裟」の色と形はその僧の位を表すものであり、儀式に合わせて取り変えられることもあります。袈裟はかつてみすぼらしい着物でしたが、日本で何世紀も経るうちに手の込んだ高価な着物となりました。

■なぜ僧は数珠を持っているのですか？

仏僧は「数珠(じゅず)」と呼ばれる珠(たま)をつなぎ合わせた紐(ひも)を持っています。数珠を手に掛けて礼拝し、また数珠を使って念仏の回数を数えます。

たいてい珠は108個付いているもの

◼ Why do priests shave their heads?

One story says that when the Buddha left his family's palace, he cut off his hair and vowed to seek the truth of existence. This may or may not be true, but a Buddhist priest shaves his head to remove any personal **adornment** and to distinguish himself from believers of other religions.

◼ What is the symbolism of a surplice (*kesa*)?

The earliest Buddhist priests were supposed to cast aside attachment to all things. They even wore clothes made of scraps of material that they could find. In China and Japan, this clothing came to be used for ceremonies. It became more colorful and luxurious. The color and shape of the surplice, *kesa*, that Japanese priests wear represents their position and may differ according to the ceremony. The *kesa* was once a poor outfit, but through the centuries in Japan, it has become a fancy, expensive garment.

◼ Why do priests carry prayer beads?

Buddhist priests carry a string of beads called *juzu*, similar to a Catholic rosary. Priests place the *juzu* over their hands when they worship. They also use these beads for counting *nembutsu*.

Usually there are 108 beads, one for each of the 108

で、それぞれが108個の煩悩に相対しています。珠の数が108の**約数**である54、36、27、18のものもあり、材料は水晶だったり木だったりすることがあります。数珠はまさに仏教徒を象徴するものです。

▣日本の仏僧は結婚できるのですか？

むかしから**仏門**に入った日本人は剃髪し、法衣(ほう え)をまとい、**独身**を通すものでした。13世紀の始め、浄土真宗の宗祖である親鸞がこのしきたりを破り、正式に結婚をした最初の仏僧となりました。親鸞以後、僧が結婚することは極めて一般的となります。1872年には、日本政府によって仏僧の結婚が合法化されました。

▣なぜそれほど多くのお寺が、家業のようにして運営されているのですか？

場合にもよりますが、お寺を家族で運営していれば住職が妻の協力を得て息子に自分の後を継がせることも可能だからです。

▣お寺はどのようにして収入を得ているのですか？

基本的には、どこのお寺も収入を**お布施**(ふ せ)に依存しています。中には「**檀家**」という信者からのものもあり、その代価として僧は読経したり儀式を執り行なったりします。故に、葬儀や法事の仕事は重要な収入源となっています。たいて

illusions or earthly passions. There are also strings with fractions of this number, including 54, 36, 27, and 18. The beads may be made of crystal or wood. This string of beads is a typical symbol of Buddhist faith.

◼ Can Japanese Buddhist priests marry?

From ancient times, Japanese who joined the **priesthood** shaved their heads, wore priest's robes and remained **celibate**. At the beginning of the 13th century, Shinran, founder of the Jodo-Shin sect, broke with these traditions. He became the first Buddhist priest to be publicly married. After Shinran, the practice became fairly common. In 1872 the Japanese government made it legal for Buddhist priests to marry.

◼ Why are so many temples run like a family business?

In some cases, the priest of a temple is assisted by his wife and he may be succeeded by his son as the head priest.

◼ How does a temple receive income?

Basically, temples depend on **donations** for income. Some donations come from the **parishioners**, *danka*, for whom the priest says prayers and carries out ceremonies. Consequently, carrying out funeral ceremonies and the series of memorial ceremonies

いの家では僧に頼んで死から七日目に**お経を上げ**てもらい、その後四十九日目まで七日毎に同様のことをしてもらいます。これによって僧にはお布施が入り、その収入が寺の維持費に当てられます。

お守りやお札などを販売して収入を得ているお寺もあれば、幼稚園を経営しているお寺もあります。規模が大きく、人気のあるところでは観光用の入場料を設定している場合もあります。

ごく稀には**托鉢**(たくはつ)をしている修行僧も見られ、たいていその僧は笠をかぶって鉢を持ったままお経を上げています。

■「檀家」の役割とはどんなものですか？

「檀家」とは、ある特定のお寺に信徒として属する家のことです。檀家はそのお寺の僧に依頼して葬式や**法要**などの儀式を執り行なってもらい、お礼にお布施をします。

江戸時代、幕府は各土地の住民におふれを出して、家毎に地元のお寺の「信徒」となるように命じました。これは民衆に当時禁止されていたキリスト教を信仰させないために行われたものであり、この際にお寺は住民を登録し管理するという役割りを果たしました。今日では、檀家はたいてい家のしきたりに従って、どこかのお寺に属し続けているものであり、その宗派の教えについてよく知っているとか、関心があるとかいったわけではありません。

is an important source. Most families ask a priest to offer prayers and **chant a sutra** seven days after death, and every seven days until the 49th day. This results in a donation to the priest which goes to the support of the temple.

Some temples have income from the sale of amulets and talismans. Some temples operate kindergartens. Large, popular temples may charge admission for sightseeing purposes.

On a rare occasion, you may see a monk **begging for alms**. Usually the monk will wear a woven straw hat and hold an alms bowl, while chanting a sutra.

◼ What is the role of *danka*?

A *danka* is a family that is affiliated to a particular temple of a Buddhist sect. The family requests the priest of that temple to perform funeral and **memorial services**. In return, the family makes donations to support the temple.

During the Edo period, the *bakufu* (military government) ordered resident families of each local neighborhood to become "members" of a local temple. This was done to make sure that people would not practice Christianity, which was banned. In this sense, Buddhist temples served as a way of registering citizens and controlling them. Today, *danka* families usually continue the family tradition of belonging to a certain temple without really knowing or caring about the specific teachings of the sect.

■仏教美術に出てくる象徴的な生き物には、どんなものがありますか？

鳳凰(ほうおう)は中国から伝わった神話の中の鳥であり、君主が**善政**をしいている時に現れると信じられていました。最も有名なものの中に、金閣寺（京都）の天辺(てっぺん)にある鳳凰と平等院（京都近郊の宇治）が所蔵している鳳凰があります。

「麒麟(きりん)」もまた君主が善政をしいている時に出現すると考えられていたものであり、ふつうの**キリン**と炎をまとった馬を掛け合わせたような姿をしています。

竜は中国における皇帝の象徴でした。日本では、天による**意志**と力を象徴するものです。

白象は仏陀の誕生にまつわるものであり、いろいろな美術品に描かれています。

孔雀(くじゃく)は想像上、恐怖や煩悩や苦しみなど毒を象徴するものを食べることが出来るとされています。

鳳凰

麒麟

竜

◾ What animal symbols appear in Buddhism iconography?

The phoenix is a mythological bird introduced from China. It was believed to appear when the ruler of a nation was **righteous**. Among the most famous are the phoenix on top of Kinkakuji (Kyoto) and the Phoenix Hall at Byodoin (Uji, near Kyoto).

The *kirin* was also thought to appear when the ruler of a country was righteous. It resembles a cross between a **giraffe** and a fiery horse.

The dragon symbolized the emperor in China. In Japan, it symbolizes the **will** and power of heaven.

The birth of Buddha is connected with a white elephant, so that animal appears in iconography.

The peacock is supposedly able to eat symbolic poisons including fear, passions and suffering.

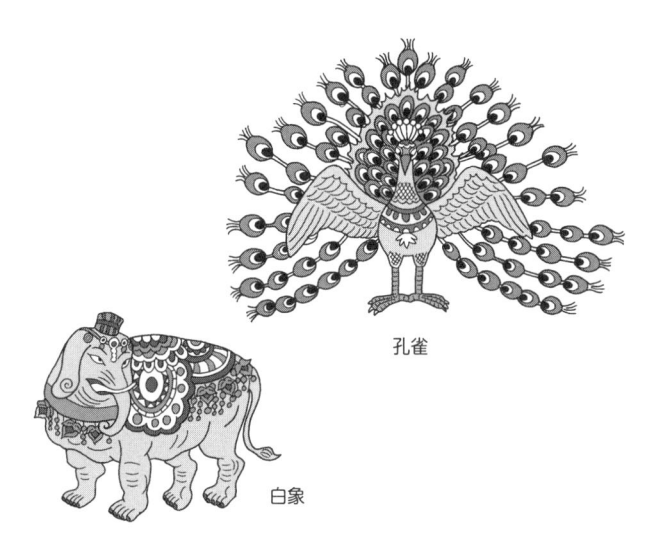

孔雀

白象

◼「千社札」とは、どんなものですか?

「千社札」とは、むかしからお寺に貼られている札のことで、表面には巡礼者の名前が書かれています。これまで、人々はお寺の門や柱にこれを貼り付けて参拝の証とし、ご利益があることを願っていました。近頃では、木の表面を傷めたり景観を損ねるという理由から、お寺側が千社札を貼ることの自粛を呼びかけています。

◼お寺では、どのようにして参拝するのですか?

神社とは異なり、お寺では拍手をせずに静かに両掌を合わせる合掌をして祈ります。「神」は呼び出す必要がありますが、仏はいつもじっとそばにいます。

◼「護摩」とはどんなものですか?

「護摩」は密教に由来するものであり、「焚く」ということを意味します。護摩において、火とは仏陀の叡智を象徴するものであり、人間の苦しみのもとである幻想や煩悩を焼き払うために用いられます。

護摩法を行う中、僧は壇の中央で護摩木を燃やし、弘法大師の像を前に祈禱を行います。祈りには特に長寿への願いが込められます。火はすべての災いを焼き尽くし、祈りはその場にいる人たちに無事と幸運をもたらします。

高野山にある寺院では、護摩会が毎朝開かれ

◼ What are *senja fuda*?

Senja fuda are traditional stickers with the name of a **pilgrim** visiting a temple. In the past, people put these on the gates or pillars of temples to show that they had made a pilgrimage to the site. They hoped to gain merit for doing so. Nowadays temples discourage the practice because it damages the surface of the wood and detracts from the appearance of the temple.

◼ How does one worship at a temple?

Unlike at a shrine, you quietly place your palms together in prayer rather than clapping. The *kami* need to be summoned, but the buddhas are always present and waiting.

◼ What is a *goma* ceremony?

The *goma* ceremony, or "fire ceremony," comes from Esoteric Buddhism. The Japanese word *goma* means "to burn." In the ceremony, fire symbolizes the wisdom of the Buddha, and is used to burn away illusion and worldly desires, the sources of human suffering.

In the ceremony, the priest burns *goma* wood in the center of a platform set up in front of an image of Kobo Daishi. Prayers are offered particularly for those who have reached critical years of their lives. The fire destroys all **calamities**, and prayers bring safety and good fortune to the participants.

The temples on Mt. Koya hold *goma* rituals every

ます。東京近郊では、平間寺とも呼ばれる川崎大師が護摩を行うことで有名です。

◾「南無阿弥陀仏」とは、どんな意味ですか？

「南無阿弥陀仏」とは「私は阿弥陀に帰依します」という意味であり、極楽浄土へ往生することを願って繰り返し唱えられます。

南無阿弥陀仏と唱える念仏は、12世紀に法然が世に広めました。その教えとは、ひたすら南無阿弥陀仏と言うことが救いへの道だというものでした。

◾「妙法蓮華経」とは、どんな意味ですか？

「南無妙法蓮華経」とは「私は妙法蓮華経に帰依します」という意味であり、日蓮宗の**題目**となっています。

◾浅草寺（浅草観音）の始まりとは、どんなものですか？

628年、浅草にいた二人の漁師が川の中から小さな観音菩薩の像を引き上げ、漁師の村の人々が小さなお寺のような場所を作って、その観音像を**安置**しました。やがてそこは有力な侍の庇護を受け、さらには徳川将軍家が祈願する寺の一つにまでなりました。浅草寺と名付けられたその寺は、人々に「浅草観音」と呼ばれて親し

morning. Nearer to Tokyo, Kawasaki Daishi temple, also called Heikenji, is well known for its *goma* ceremony.

◼ What is the meaning of *"Namu Amida Butsu"*?

The chant *"Namu Amida Butsu"* means "I believe in Amida Buddha." It is chanted in the hope of being reborn in the Pure Land of Amida.

The practice was popularized by Honen in the 12th century. He taught that just saying this was the best path to salvation.

◼ What is the meaning of *"Myoho Renge-kyo"*?

The chant *"Namu Myoho Renge-kyo"* means "I believe in the Lotus Sutra." It is the *daimoku* or **mantra** of the Nichiren sect of Buddhism.

◼ What is the origin of Senso-ji (Asakusa Kannon)?

In 628 two fishermen in Asakusa pulled out of the river a small image of the Kannon Bodhisattva. The people of their village made a small temple to **house** it. Eventually the temple received support from important samurai and it even became one of the family temples of the Tokugawa shoguns. Named Sensoji and popularly called "Asakusa Kannon," it was rebuilt to become a

まれ、建て替えられて町の人たちが多く訪れる大寺院となりました。浅草寺は第二次世界大戦で破壊され、本堂が1958年に再建されました。

浅草寺は年明け最初の参拝である「初詣で」の場所として人気があります。7月10日には「ほおずき市」と呼ばれる伝統的な催し物の会場となり、人々が**ほおずき**を買い求めます。

> 「ほおずき市」とともににぎわうのが「四万六千日」という縁日。この日に参詣すると4万6000日参詣したのと同じ功徳があるといわれている。

◨ 浅草寺の門はなぜ「雷門」と呼ばれるのですか？

「雷の門」とは言いますが、実のところこの大きな門は「風神と雷神の門」です。正式名称は「風雷神門」であり、「風」は風神、「雷」は雷神を指しています。この二神は邪悪なものを寄せ付けない恐ろしい表情をしており、火事やその他自然災害からお寺を護ると考えられています。もとからあった門は1865年に焼失し、1960年に新しい門が再建されました。

門の内側には「仲見世」という250メートルの商店街があり、みやげ物や食べ物を売る店が

浅草寺（東京都）

large temple visited by many townsmen. The temple was destroyed in World War II and the main building was rebuilt in 1958.

The temple is a popular place to visit for *hatsumode*, the first visit to a temple or shrine at the New Year. On July 10, it is the site of a traditional fair called *Hozuki Ichi*, where people buy *hozuki*, **Chinese lantern plants**.

◩ Why is the gate called "*Kaminari-mon*"?

Kaminari-mon means "Thunder Gate," but the official name of this large gate is "Gate of the Thunder Deity and the Wind Deity." Its formal name is *Furaijin-mon*. *Fu* is for *Fujin*, the god of the winds. *Rai* is for *Raijin*, the god of thunder. The two gods have fierce expressions which keep evil away. They are thought to protect the temple from fire and other natural disasters. The original gate burned down in 1865, and the new gate was rebuilt in 1960.

Inside the gate is *Nakamise*, a 250-meter arcade filled with souvenir shops and shops selling food. Originally many of these were tea shops and small food shops providing refreshment to temple visitors.

軒を連ねています。もともとこれらの多くは参拝客に軽食などを出す茶屋でした。

■参拝客は、なぜ浅草寺で線香を上げるのですか?

参拝客は、お供えとして線香を上げ、お清めとして煙を自分に扇（あお）ぎかけます。

■成田山（新勝寺）

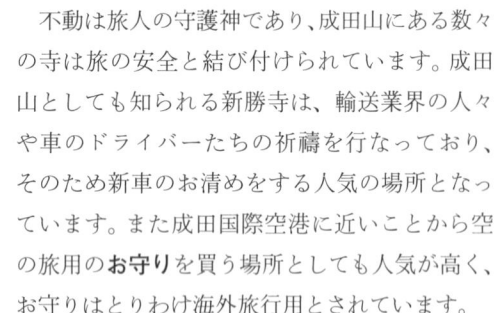

不動は旅人の守護神であり、成田山にある数々の寺は旅の安全と結び付けられています。成田山としても知られる新勝寺は、輸送業界の人々や車のドライバーたちの祈禱を行なっており、そのため新車のお清めをする人気の場所となっています。また成田国際空港に近いことから空の旅用の**お守り**を買う場所としても人気が高く、お守りはとりわけ海外旅行用とされています。

成田山新勝寺（千葉県）

■鎌倉大仏

この巨大な青銅の阿弥陀仏像は1252年に鋳（ちゅう）造（ぞう）が開始されていますが、正確な日付は不明です。始めのうちは大きなお堂に納められていたものの、その建物は1495年に消失してしまいました。おそらく火事、もしくは地震、台風、津波などによるものです。

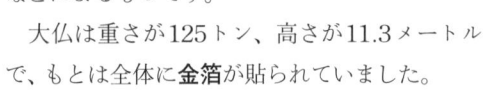

大仏は重さが125トン、高さが11.3メートルで、もとは全体に**金箔**が貼られていました。

鎌倉大仏（神奈川県）

◼ Why do visitors burn incense at Sensoji?

Visitors light sticks of incense as offerings and wave smoke over themselves as a ritual act of purification.

◼ Narita-san (Shinshoji)

Dedicated to Fudo Myoo, the guardian of travelers, affiliated Narita-san temples throught Japan are associated with travel safety. The head temple, Shinshoji, is located in Narita city, from which it takes its nickname, Narita-san. It receives prayers from people involved in the transport industry and from car drivers. As a result, it is a popular place to have a new car purified. Because it is near Narita International Airport, it is also a popular place to buy **amulets** for air travel in general and overseas travel in particular.

◼ Kamakura Daibutsu

Casting of this enormous bronze image of Vairocana Buddha began in 1252, but its completion date is not clear. Originally it was housed in a great hall, but that structure was lost in 1495, possibly by fire, earthquake, typhoon or tsunami.

The statue weighs 125 tons, measures 11.3 meters (37.1 feet) high, and was originally covered in **gold leaf**.

◾清水寺

清水寺(京都府)

清水寺は、延鎮和尚によって798年に開かれました。延鎮は山中の水場(「清水」)で水行をしている隠者に出会ったと言われています。延鎮は観音僧を彫り、坂上田村麻呂とともに清水寺の始まりとなるものを造ってその仏像を納めました。そして810年、清水寺は鎮護国家の道場として選ばれました。この寺院は火事や地震や戦によって何度も壊れ落ちています。現在の建物はほとんどが1633年から存在しているものです。

寺の名前にもなっている「清水」は、今でも清水の舞台下方にある滝から流れています。かつてそこは苦行の場でした。今日では、観光客が順番にその水の味を体験しています。

清水寺の本堂裏にある神社は地主神社といい、二人の男女を結び付けて恋愛を成就させる「縁結び」で有名です。社務所では、縁結びのお守りが販売されています。

◾銀閣寺(慈照寺)

足利義政は歴代室町将軍の一人として1449年から1479年の間その地位に君臨していました。実際のところ義政は政治よりも文化に興味を持っていた人で、金閣寺(1397年)に感化されて京都の東山に壮麗な山荘を建てる計画をしました。建物の壁にはすべて銀箔を貼る予定でしたが、それが完成する前に義政はこの世を去ってしまいました。それでもその建物は銀閣と呼

銀閣寺(京都府)

◉ Kiyomizu-dera

Kiyomizu-dera was founded in 798 by the Buddhist priest Enchin. It is said that Enchin met a **hermit** carrying out religious practices near a spring of pure water (*kiyomizu*) in the mountains. Enchin carved an image of Kannon and, with Sakanoue no Tamuramaro, built the first temple to house the image. In 810 Kiyomizu-dera was chosen as a temple where people offered prayers for the protection of the country. The temple was destroyed by fire, earthquake and warfare many times. Most of the current buildings date from 1633.

The "pure water" which gives the temple its name still comes from a waterfall below the temple's main balcony. It was once a place for **ascetic practices**. Nowadays tourists **take turns** tasting the water.

The Shinto shrine behind the main hall of Kiyomizu-dera is Jishu Shrine. It is famous for *enmusubi*, linking two people together as a couple. The shrine office sells talismans for that purpose.

◉ Ginkaku-ji (Jisho-ji)

Although Ashikaga Yoshimasa ruled as one of the Muromachi shoguns between 1449 and 1479, he was more interested in culture than in government. Influenced by Kinkakuji, the Golden Pavilion (1397), he planned a splendid **villa** in the Higashiyama section of Kyoto. He planned to cover its walls with **silver leaf**, but he died before it was completed. However, the building is referred to as the Silver Pavilion. It is now

ばれ、現在は慈照寺という名前の禅寺となっています。

◼ 金閣寺（鹿苑寺）

金閣寺は、かつて公家に所有されていた山荘が第三代将軍足利義満の政治拠点となったものです。義満は10年を費やして、その山荘を優雅な**隠居後の御所**へと変えました。義満の死後にそこは禅寺となり、正式に鹿苑寺と名付けられました。

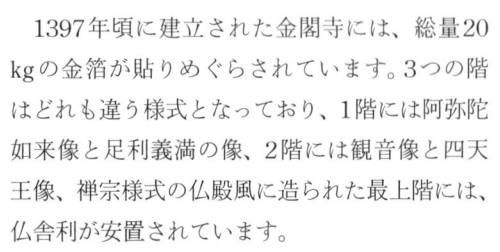

金閣寺（京都府）

1397年頃に建立された金閣寺には、総量20kgの金箔が貼りめぐらされています。3つの階はどれも違う様式となっており、1階には阿弥陀如来像と足利義満の像、2階には観音像と四天王像、禅宗様式の仏殿風に造られた最上階には、仏舎利が安置されています。

金閣寺は錯乱した一人の学僧によって1950年に放火され破壊されました。現在の建物は1955年に再建されたものです。1987年の改修では、さらに20万枚の金箔が追加されました。

◼ 三十三間堂（蓮華王院 れんげおういん）

この長い建物は三十三間堂と呼ばれていますが、それは柱で等間隔に区切られた「三十三」の「間」があるからです。ここには「千手観音」が1001体納められています。これらは12世紀から13世紀の間に制作されたもので、繰り返し信仰を形にすることによってのみ救われるという信念から彫られました。

三十三間堂（京都府）

a Zen temple named Jishoji.

◼ Kinkaku-ji (Rokuon-ji)

Once the villa of a court noble, Kinkakuji became the political base of the third Ashikaga shogun, Yoshimitsu. He spent ten years turning it into an elegant **retreat**. After he died, it became a Zen temple, officially named Rokuonji.

The Golden Pavilion, built in 1397, is covered with 20 kilograms of gold leaf. Each of its three floors has a different design. The first floor has images of Amida and Yoshimitsu. The second floor has an image of Kannon and Shitenno. The top floor, build in the style of a Zen temple, has relics of the Buddha.

The pavilion was destroyed in 1950 by a deranged monk. The current building was reproduced in 1955. Repairs in 1987 added 200,000 sheets of gold leaf.

◼ Sanjusangendo (Rengeoin)

This long building is called Sanjusangendo because it has 33 (*sanjusan*) bays (*gen*, or *ken*) which are separated by evenly spaced pillars. It houses 1,001 Thousand-armed Kannon (*Senju Kannon*). They were carved during the 12th and 13th centuries from the belief that people could win salvation only by repeated acts of devotion.

建物の全長は120メートルほどあります。33という数字は、**慈悲**の仏である観音が全人類を救うため変化する回数を象徴しています。

◾ 東大寺

奈良時代（710-794）、仏教は総じて朝廷と国家の宗教として確立されました。次々と起こる疫病、自然災害、飢饉、そして**世の中の不穏な出来事**によって、聖武天皇は自国の安定に不安を抱くようになります。743年、聖武天皇は安寧と**繁栄**を確固たるものにしようと毘盧舎那大仏建立の詔を出し、仏の加護が国全体に及ぶことを願いました。その青銅の大仏は752年に完成し、「奈良大仏」として知られています。

東大寺大仏殿（奈良県）

高さ約15メートルほどの大仏は何度も破損しては復興されました。当初の寺院にあった建造物は大部分が破壊され、その中には大仏殿も含まれています。現在の建物は1709年に落成したものであり、一般に世界最大の**木造建築物**とされています。それでも、大きさは当初の八分の五しかありません。

また東大寺の周辺には、正倉院と二月堂という二つの重要な建物があります。正倉院は木造の**倉庫**で、本来は8世紀のむかしから数千点の美術品が納められていた宝物庫でした。ここに保管されていた宝物には、日本、中国、果てはギ

The building is 120 meters (394 feet) long. The number 33 is symbolic of the number of times Kannon, the deity of **mercy**, changed form in order to bring salvation to all humankind.

◼ Todai-ji

During the Nara period (710–794), the capital was in Nara and Buddhism was established as the religion of the imperial court and the country as a whole. A series of epidemics, natural disasters, famines and **social unrest** led Emperor Shomu to worry about the stability of his government. To establish peace and **prosperity**, in 743 he called for the casting of a giant Birushana (Vairocana) Buddha so that the blessings of the Buddha would spread across all of Japan. The bronze statue was completed in 752 and is known as the Great Buddha of Nara, or *Nara Daibutsu*.

The 15-meter-high statue has been repeatedly damaged and restored. Most of the original temple buildings were destroyed, including the building that housed the Great Buddha. The current building, completed in 1709, is generally considered the largest **wooden structure** in the world. Yet, it is only five-eighths the size of the original building.

On the grounds are two other important buildings, the Shosoin and the Nigatsudo. The Shosoin is a wooden **storehouse** that originally housed several thousand fine objects of art from the 8th century. The treasures that were stored in this imperial warehouse

リシャを代表する名品が含まれています。現在それらの品々は奈良国立博物館で保存され、毎年秋には展示会が開かれます。

■「お水取り」とはどんなものですか？

東大寺の修行僧たちは、観音に罪を**懺悔**するという宗教行事を二月堂で行います。この行事は3月1日から14日まで通して続けられ、期間中の**見どころ**となるのは夜に行われる「お松明」です。僧たちが燃え盛る巨大な**松明**を持ち、何かを唱えながら本道の舞台を欄干に沿って次々と走って行きます。その松明から降る火の粉は悪霊を追い払うと言い伝えられています。この夜に行われる豪快な火のお清めは、多くの**観客**を呼ぶ催し物となっています。行事は13日目の未明、「お水取り」をもって終了します。汲み上げられた聖水は観音に供えられ、その場にいる人たちに分け与えられます。

■法隆寺（奈良近郊）

法隆寺は607年に最初の落成を迎え、670年に火事で全焼しました。現在の建物は711年頃から存在しているものです。法隆寺は日本で最初に世界遺産として登録された場所です。

五重塔は7世紀の終わり頃から存在しているもので、国内最古の仏塔となっています。「金堂」は日本で最も古い木造建築であり、そこには三体の見事な仏像（釈迦如来、薬師如来、阿弥陀

include masterpieces from Japan, China and as far away as Greece. The items are now stored at the Nara National Museum and selections are on view every autumn.

▣ What is *Omizutori*?

Monks at Todaiji conduct rituals of **repentance** to Kannon at Nigatsudo. The rituals continue from March 1st through 14th. A **highlight** of this period is the burning of *otaimatsu*, torches, at the Nigatsudo at night. Priests race along the outside balcony of the temple chanting and carrying huge burning **torches**. Tradition says that the shower of sparks that fall from the torches chases away evil spirits. This nightly event is a dynamic example of purification by fire and draws large numbers of **spectators**. The ritual comes to an end early on the 13th with the "drawing of sacred water," *omizutori*. This sacred water is offered to Kannon and to the attending spectators.

▣ Horyuji (near Nara)

The first Horyuji temple was completed in 607, but it was completely destroyed by fire in 670. The current temple dates from about 711. It is the first site in Japan to be registered as a World Heritage Site.

The **five-story pagoda** dates from the end of the 7th century and is the oldest pagoda in the country. The Golden Hall, *Kondo*, is the oldest wooden building in Japan. It contains three magnificent images of Buddha

如来)が日本最古の四天王像に囲まれて安置されています。八角形の「夢殿」という建物には聖徳太子の像が納められており、春と秋のわずかな期間にだけ公開されます。

◼ なぜ仏教徒は火葬し、遺骨をお墓に入れるのですか？

仏教が到来する前、日本人は**土葬**をしていました。彼らは死者が生き返って生者に災いすると信じており、故に死体が二度と起き上がらないようにしたいと思っていました。

仏教が到来した後に、法相宗を日本に広めた道昭という名の僧が自分を**火葬**にして欲しいと遺言しました。道昭は日本で最初に火葬された人物だと考えられています。

日本人はやがて、火葬という習わしに**遺骨**を墓石に納めるということを組み合わせました。始めは社会のエリートたちだけがこれを行なっていましたが、江戸時代初頭には一般の人々へと広まりました。現在、死者の99パーセントが火葬され、遺骨が**骨壺**に納められます。骨壺の多くは自家の墓に納骨され、先祖や他の家族のものとともに安置されます。最近は土地を見付けるのが大変なので、多数の遺骨を安置できる背高の**納骨壇**もあります。

◼ 死後、「法事」は何回行われるのですか？

法事は発祥地のインドにおいては七回とされ、

(Shaka, Yakushi and Amida), surrounded by the oldest Four Heavenly Kings in Japan. The octagonal Hall of Dreams, *Yume-dono*, contains an image of Shotoku Taishi, which is displayed briefly in spring and autumn.

◼ Why do Buddhists cremate and put the remains in a grave?

Before Buddhism arrived, the Japanese **buried the dead**. They believed that the dead would return to life and cause problems for the living. Therefore, they wanted to be sure the body could not rise up again.

When Buddhism arrived, the founder of the Hosso sect, named Dosho, requested that his body be **cremated**. He is thought to be the first person cremated in Japan.

The Japanese eventually combined the custom of cremation with the setting up of a monument covering the **remains**. In the beginning only the elite did this, but beginning in the Edo period the custom spread to ordinary people. Currently, 99% of the deceased are cremated and ashes are placed in a **funerary urn**. Most urns are placed in the family tomb, with those of earlier generations or other family members. Because land is hard to find, there are now vertical **mausolea** where the ashes of large numbers of people can be kept.

◼ How many memorial services, *hoji*, are held after death?

The Buddhist custom that came from India was to

死後七日目から四十九日目までの間に行われていました。中国において百ヵ日、一回忌、三回忌が加えられ、そして日本で十三回忌、十七回忌、二十三回忌、三十三回忌が加わりました。

◧「仏壇」とは、どんなものですか?

「仏壇」とは小さな飾り戸棚のようなもので、中には仏像や先祖の「**位牌**」が安置されます。たいてい仏壇には、**蝋燭**、**香炉**、鈴、小型の掛け軸、もしくは像などが置いてあり、家によっては故人の遺影が飾られている場合もあります。家の人たちは折りあるごとにご飯とお水をお供えし、線香と蝋燭を灯し、鈴を鳴らし、両掌を合わせ「**合掌**」をしながら祈ります。

◧「位牌」とは、どんなものですか?

「位牌」には、故人の**戒名**が記されています。宗派によってはサンスクリット語の文字や宗派名、寺院の名前が書いてある場合もあります。一般に死から最初の四十九日間には白木の位牌が用いられます。そしてその期間が過ぎた後、多くの場合は黒塗りの新しい位牌が作られて、それが家の**仏壇**に安置されます。

hold seven memorial services. These were held between the seventh and forty-ninth days after death. Chinese Buddhists added a service on the 100th day, the first anniversary and the third anniversary. Japanese Buddhists added services on the 13th, 17th, 23rd and 33rd anniversaries.

◼ What is a *butsudan*?

A *butsudan* is a small cabinet containing an image of Buddha and **memorial tablets**, *ihai*, for the family ancestors. Generally, the cabinet has candles, an **incense burner**, a bell and a small scroll or statue. Some families also put a photograph of the departed. Often the family makes an offering of rice and water, lights incense and a candle, rings the small bell and **places the palms of the hands together** in prayer in what is called *gassho*.

◼ What is a memorial tablet?

A memorial tablet, *ihai*, has the **posthumous Buddhist name** of the deceased person written on it. Depending on the sect, it may also have Sanskrit characters, the name of the sect or the name of the temple. Generally, for the first 49 days following death, the tablet is plain wood. After that period has passed, a new one is made which is often painted or varnished black. It is kept in the **Buddhist altar** in the home.

■なぜ死者には戒名が与えられるのですか？

　本来「戒名」とは、仏僧となった者に与えられるものでした。それは名を授かった者が仏陀の教えを信仰し、その教えに従うと約束したことを表しています。日本仏教では誰もが仏になる力を持っているとされていますが、誰もが僧になるというわけではありません。そこで、死後にはこのように戒名が与えられることになっています。

■「卒塔婆」とは、どんなものですか？

　これらの卒塔婆といわれる「板塔婆」は墓所に置かれるものです。表側には戒名や経文が記されています。文字に使用されているのはサンスクリット語（梵字）であり、仏教を日本に伝える際に用いられた**宗教用言語**の一つです。裏側には寄贈者の名前が書かれる場合もあります。

　これらの板は1メートルから2メートルくらいの長さで、故人の墓に立てて置かれます。墓自体は家族全員のためにあるものですが、「卒塔婆」は故人ひとりの冥福を祈って供えられます。板の中にあるそれぞれの形には、下から順に、地、水、火、風、空といった五大要素の意味が盛り込まれています。石塔婆のそれぞれの石も、同じ意味合いを持っています。

■「お盆」とはどんな日なのですか？

　「お盆」は最も重要な仏教の**年中行事**です。それは仏教における死者の祭りであり、8月の12

◼ Why are the dead given Buddhist names?

Originally, the *kaimyo*, an ordination name, was a name given to a person when he or she became a Buddhist priest. It showed that the person has faith in the teachings of Buddha and promised to follow them. Japanese Buddhism says that everyone has the potential for becoming a buddha. But not everyone becomes a priest. So people are given this kind of ordination name after death.

◼ What is a *sotoba*?

These narrow wooden planks (*sotoba*) are placed at graves. On the front is written a posthumous Buddhist name or a scripture. The characters are written in Sanskrit, one of the **sacred languages** used to transmit Buddhism to Japan. On the back may be written the name of the donor.

These planks range from one to two meters in length and are placed upright at the tomb. The tomb itself is for the whole family, but the *sotoba* is offered for the repose of the deceased individual. The shape of each *sotoba*, from the bottom, has five divisions, representing the five elements: earth, water, fire, wind and air. One type of traditional gravestone has the same five divisions.

◼ What happens at *O-bon*?

O-bon, the Bon Festival, is the most important **annual event** of the Buddhist calendar. It is the Buddhist

日から16日まで続きます。伝統的な期間は7月12日から16日であり、まだこの時期をお盆としている地域もあります。

家庭では「盆棚」と呼ばれる祭壇を用意します。これは先祖の霊がお盆の間とどまるためのものです。盆棚には、きゅうりやなすに**楊枝**の脚をつけて作った牛や馬の小さな人形を供えます。この動物たちは先祖の霊を運ぶものとしての象徴です。また、花や果物、線香、蝋燭などが供えられることもあります。

8月12日の晩には、帰ってくる死者の魂を迎えるために家の玄関で小さな火を灯すことがあります。この火は「迎え火」と呼ばれ、地域によっては火の代わりに盆ちょうちんが灯されます。8月13日からが実際のお盆となります。8月16日には死者の魂を送り出すために同様の火が焚かれ、こちらは「送り火」と呼ばれています。京都の五山送り火はこの習わしの有名な例です。

■ 曼荼羅とは、どんなものですか？

曼荼羅とは**仏教的宇宙観**を描いた絵であり、難解な考えを視覚化することによって把握し易くするものです。曼荼羅は**左右を対称として**象徴的に宇宙を論じており、たいてい四種類の像、即ち如来、菩薩、明王、天部の間にある関係を表しています。二つの主要な曼荼羅に、「金剛界曼荼羅」と「胎蔵界曼荼羅」があります。真言宗には、これら二つの曼荼羅間の動的関係を表す儀式が存在します。

Festival of the Dead and it lasts from the 12th through the 16th of August. The traditional period, still observed in some regions, is July 12th through 16th.

Families prepare an altar called a *bon-dana*. This is for the spirits of the ancestors to stay during the festival. On the altar are placed small figures of cows and horses made of cucumbers and eggplants with legs made from **toothpicks**. These symbolize the animals that carry the spirits. The family may also place flowers, fresh fruit, incense and candles on the altar.

On the evening of August 12, families may light a small fire at the door of their home in order to welcome back the souls of the departed. These small fires are called *mukaebi*. In some regions, a special paper lantern is lit instead. August 13th is the actual day of *O-bon*. A similar fire is lit on August 16th to send the souls off, and this is called *okuribi*. The Gozan no Okuribi in Kyoto is a famous example of this custom.

◨ What is a mandala?

Mandala, *mandara*, are paintings that reprensent the **Buddhist universe**. They make complex ideas easier to grasp by making these ideas visual. They are **symmetrical** symbolic cosmologies that usually show the relations between four kinds of images: buddhas, bodhisattvas, myoo and tembu. The two main mandalas are the Diamond (Kongo-kai) and the Womb (Taizo-kai) mandalas. The Shingon sect has rituals showing the dynamic relationships between these two mandalas.

平面に描かれた曼荼羅の他に、別の形式で表現された曼荼羅もあります。とりわけ密教においては、仏堂に安置されたいくつもの仏像で一つの曼荼羅を形成している例が見られます。

　神道にもまた曼荼羅は存在し、中には神道と仏教を組み合わせたようなものもあります。最も有名なものは熊野三神社の曼荼羅です。その他神道の曼荼羅には、鳥の目から見たような神社境内の風景を描いたものもあります。

■京都の「五山送り火」とはどんなものですか?

　「送り火」とはお盆が終わる日の晩に儀式として灯される火のことであり、死者の霊を**冥府**への帰りの途に送り出すものとされています。

　8月16日には、「五山送り火」が京都で催されます。市街地周辺の山々には漢字などを象ったかがり火が灯され、死者の霊を導きます。かがり火には、漢字の形に灯るものが「大」と「妙法」(仏教の経典名)の二つ、そして(先祖を送り返すための)「船」、「鳥居」の形のものが一つずつです。この伝統的行事の始まりは室町時代までさかのぼります。

©中田昭

如意が岳＝大文字
大北山＝左大文字
松が崎西山・東山＝妙法
明見山＝船形
曼荼羅山＝鳥居形

In addition to the two-dimensional mandala paintings, there is another variety. The statues of the Buddhas in a worship hall may form a mandala, particularly in Esoteric Buddhism.

Shinto also has mandalas, some of which are combinations of Shinto and Buddhism. The most famous is found in three shrines of Kumano. Other Shinto mandalas show a bird's-eye view of a shrine in its natural setting.

◢ What is the *okuribi* of the Gozan in Kyoto?

Okuribi ("sending off fires") are ceremonial fires that are lit on the evening of the last day of *O-bon*. They are supposed to send the spirits of the dead on their way back to the **underworld**.

On August 16, the Gozan Farewell Bonfire (*Gozan no okuribi*) is held in Kyoto. On mountains around the city, bonfires shaped like Chinese characters are lit to guide the spirits of the dead. They are two bonfires with the character for "great" (*dai*), one with the two characters "*Myoho*" (the name of a Buddhist sutra), and one each with the shapes of a ship (to carry the ancestors back) and a *torii*. The tradition of this bonfire dates back to the Muromachi period.

◼「彼岸」とはどんなものですか？

　一年に二度あるこの仏事は日本の仏教に特有のものです。その**一週間にわたる**期間は「彼岸」と呼ばれ、**春分**と**秋分**を中日としています。彼岸には中日とその前後三日間が含まれます。この二つの期間中に仏教徒の人たちは参拝をするものであり、どこの家族も彼岸の「墓参り」をして先祖に敬意を表します。

　仏教の「彼岸」という言葉は「向こう岸」、もしくは涅槃という意味です。

◼「墓参り」とは、どんなものですか？

　彼岸や盆、またそれ以外の時期でも家人は先祖の墓所を訪れます。彼らはバケツに入った水を持参して墓石を掃除し、墓の周りの**雑草を取**り、その辺のゴミを拾います。それから花と線香を供えて**祈ります**。

◼「花祭」とは、どんなものですか？

　「花祭」とはお釈迦さまの誕生日を祝うものであり、毎年4月8日に行われます。花を飾りつけた小さな祭壇（「花御堂」）を作り、そこに誕生仏という像を置きます。この像は片方の手を天に向け、もう片方を地に向けており、これによって天上天下唯我独尊ということを表しています。人々はその像に「甘茶」などをかけて祝います。この伝統行事は、お釈迦さまが誕生した時に竜が天から降りてきて香水をかけたという話に由

◼ What is *higan*?

This twice-a-year celebration is special to Japanese Buddhism. The **weeklong** periods called *higan* center on the **spring equinox** and the **autumn equinox**. *Higan* includes the equinox, the three days before it and the three days after it. During these two periods, Buddhist services are performed. Families visit the family grave, *haka mairi*, during these periods to pay their respects to their ancestors.

The word *higan* in Buddhism means "the other shore," or Nirvana.

◼ What is *haka mairi*?

At *higan*, *O-bon* and other times through the year, family members visit the graves of their ancestors. They bring water in a bucket to clean the **tombstone**. They **weed** around it and pick up any trash they find. Then they offer flowers and incense and **offer a prayer**.

◼ What is *hana matsuri*?

Hana Matsuri, the Flower Festival, celebrates the birthday of the Buddha. It is held every year on April 8. A small altar decorated with flowers (*hanami-do*) is created. On it is placed a statue of Buddha as a child. This figure points one hand toward heaven and the other toward earth. This symbolizes that he is honored in both places. People pour water or sweet tea (*amacha*) on the statue to honor him. This tradition comes from the story that at Buddha's birth, dragons descended

来しています。花祭は、「灌仏会」とも呼ばれています。

■「千日回峰行」とはどんなものですか?

文字通り「千日歩く」という「千日回峰行」は比叡山における天台宗の苦行であり、7年間にわたって行われます。修行僧は身を清めた後に6時間から7時間続く夜間の巡拝を始め、山の霊場を巡って神社や木や岩や滝や道端の像の前で礼拝をします。そして早朝に戻ってくると、他の僧たちと同じく**日々の行**に取り掛かります。夜には3時間しか眠りません。これを100日**続けて**行います。

1、2、3年目には毎日35kmから40kmを歩きます。4、5年目には100日間の行を2度行い、6年目には夜毎60km。7年目には84kmに増やしてそれを100日間、そして30kmから40kmでもう100日間。合計すると、7年間で3万8000kmから4万6000kmを歩くことになります。この終わりには最後を締めくくる9日間の、断食、断水、不眠、不臥の行が待っています。

これを終えた行者はほんのわずかしかいませんが、最近の記録では天台宗の僧侶、酒井雄哉が1980年と1987年の2度成し遂げています。

from heaven and poured scented water on him. *Hana Matsuri* is also called *kanbutsu-e*.

▣ What is *sennichi kaihogyo*?

Literally "thousand-day practice of walking," the *sennichi kaihogyo*, is an ascetic practice of the Tendai sect on Mt. Hiei. The practice takes place over a period of seven years. The monk purifies himself before beginning a six or seven hour nighttime circuit. He visits sacred locations on the mountain, praying and chanting before Buddhist temples, Shinto shrines, trees, rocks, waterfalls and roadside statues. When he returns early in the morning, he begins his **daily chores** like other monks. At night, he sleeps only three hours. He does this for 100 days **in succession**.

During the 1st, 2nd and 3rd year, he travels 35 to 40 kilometers every day. In the 4th and 5th years, he does two periods of 100 days. In the 6th year he travels 60 kilometers each night. In the 7th year he steps up the pace to 84 kilometers for 100 days and then 30 to 40 kilometers for another 100 days. He totals between 38,000 and 46,000 kilometers over seven years. At the end of this he faces a final period of nine days without sleeping, without lying down, without eating and without drinking.

Few have completed this practice, but the Tendai priest, Sakai Yusai completed it twice, once in 1980 and again in 1987.

◼「即身成仏」とはどんなものですか?

真言宗は「**即身成仏**」、つまり「人は仏と一体になることができる」と教えています。これは、人は生きながらにして究極の悟りを得ることができるということを意味します。そして即身成仏とは精神的過程であるとともに、肉体的過程でもあると考えられています。

これについて珍しい例が鶴岡(山形県)の海向寺に見られます。かつて僧だった人がまだ生きている間に食を断ち、座って瞑想したままの状態で**葬られて**いました。僧のミイラ化した死体は後に掘り出され、僧衣を着せられて海向寺に祀られています。

◼人はなぜ四国八十八箇所巡礼(じゅんれい)をするのですか?

「四国遍路」、または「四国八十八箇所巡礼」とは特定の88ヵ所を経由して行う巡礼のことです。どのようにしてこの巡礼が行われるようになったのかははっきりしていません。しかしながら巡礼する場所は、弘法大師としても知られる空海と何かしらの関係があると考えられています。空海は四国の善通寺市で生まれ、中国で学んだ後に高野山で真言宗を開きました。四国は空海の「**本拠地**」なだけに、その**熱狂的崇拝者**が増えてもふしぎではありません。

四国島を回るその巡礼は1400kmに及ぶもので、それには真言宗の寺院が80ヵ所と他宗派のものが8ヵ所含まれています。一般に巡礼者の

◼ What is *sokushin jobutsu*?

Shingon (Esoteric) Buddhism teaches that "**one can become a buddha in the present body**" (*sokushin jobutsu*). This means one can gain perfect enlightenment in one's present lifetime. It is considered a physical process as well as a spiritual process.

One unique form of this is found at Kaikoji temple in Tsuruoka (Yamagata prefecture). A former priest, while still alive, refrained from eating and **was interred** in a position of seated mediation. His mummified body was later disinterred. His remains, clothed in priest's garments, are worshipped in the temple.

◼ Why do people undertake the Shikoku 88-temple pilgrimage?

The "Shikoku pilgrimage," *Shikoku henro* or *Shikoku hachijuhakkasho*, is a route that links 88 specific places of worship. There is no clear explanation of how this pilgrimage developed. However, the places are believed to have some connection with Kukai, also known as Kobo Daishi. Kukai was born in Zentsuji, in Shikoku, and after studying in China, he established Shingon Buddhism on Mt. Koya. His "home ground" was Shikoku, so it is not surprising that a **cult** devoted to him developed there.

The pilgrimage, which circles the island of Shikoku, is 1,400 kilometers (870 miles) long. It includes eighty Shingon temples and eight temples of other sects. In

最も多い春には、天気が良い場合で一周するのに6週間ほどかかります。通常は時計回りに進みますが、それは個人の自由であり、反時計回りをしても、**区画毎に**回っても、一度にやり遂げても、一年かけても構いません。最近では、大勢の参加者たちがツアーバスを利用して10日から12日間で回っています。

　伝統的な装いとして身に着けられているものには白衣、菅笠（すげがさ）、木の杖などがあります。白衣は自分が**俗世**を離れた特別な状態にあることを表し、杖は巡礼の間ずっと共にある弘法大師の魂を象徴しています。一人道中もいれば、「先達（せんだつ）」と呼ばれる引率者について回る団体もいます。先達とは場所ごとの説明をし、各場での礼拝に際して先導をする人のことです。それぞれの寺院では、「納経帳（のうきょうちょう）」と呼ばれる専用の帳面に、僧からその寺の「**朱印**」をもらうことができ、また毛筆で文字も書き足してもらえます。

　四国遍路を思い立つ動機は多岐にわたっており、巡礼者は真言宗信者でなくとも構いません。個人的な理由から参加する人たちもおり、それは健康を取り戻すためとか、挫折して内省したりとか、人生を模索したりとかさまざまです。1990年代には、「リストラ」されて人生に新たな意味を見出そうとしている中年男性が次第に増えていきました。そして今はまた純粋な観光客が主流となっています。彼らが求めるものは、歴史と信仰がうまく組み合わさったツアーを体

good weather—spring is most common—it takes six weeks to walk the entire route. The usual route is clockwise. However, one is free to go counter-clockwise, do it **in sections**, complete it all at one time, or spread it over a period of years. Large numbers of participants now travel the route by tour bus in ten to twelve days.

Traditional clothing includes a white shirt, a bamboo hat, and a wooden staff. The white shirt symbolizes the special condition of withdrawal from the **everyday world**. The staff symbolizes the spirit of Kobo Daishi which accompanies the pilgrim at all times. Some individuals travel alone, while others travel in large groups conducted by a leader called a *sendatsu*, who tells about each place and leads the worship at each location. At each temple, the pilgrim can have a priest put the **temple's seal** (*shuin*) in a special pilgrim's book called a *nokyocho*. The priest also adds some calligraphy in black ink.

Motivations for setting out on the pilgrimage vary widely, and the pilgrims are not necessarily followers of Shingon Buddhism. Some join for personal reasons, such as regaining health, reflecting on a failure, or seeking a path in life. In the 1990s, they increasingly included middle-aged men who had been "restructured" and were trying to find new meaning in their lives. Then again a large number are simply tourists. They want to enjoy a traditional natural setting with a historical, religious twist.

験しながら、伝統漂う環境を満喫することです。

◾ 他には、どんな巡礼があるのですか？

最もよく知られているのは西日本における西国巡礼であり、観音像を所蔵している寺院33ヵ所を経由するというものです。この数字が持つ重要な意味は、観音が33変化して苦しむ者を皆救うということにあります。観音はそれを妙法蓮華経の中で明言しています。巡礼は和歌山県にある那智山に始まり、途中あちこちへと迂回しながら琵琶湖の東方にある地へと辿り着きます。

他にも「散歩」感覚で楽しめる、「七福神めぐり」という寺社巡りがあります。東京では、水天宮を含む日本橋界隈などが人気のコースです。

◾「あみだくじ」は、なぜそう呼ばれるのですか？

日本の人々は、時々ある種のくじ引きをして勝者を決めることがあります。一人が**格子模様**のようなものを紙に描き、くじを引く人各々がそれに一本ずつ線を書き入れて勝つ人を決めます。この模様は阿弥陀仏の**後光**と似ており、そこからこの「くじ引き」は「あみだくじ」と呼ばれています。このようにしてくじを引くことを、**神さま仏さまの言う通り**、というふうに言います。

◼ What other pilgrimages are there?

The best known is the Saikoku pilgrimage in western Japan. It links 33 temples housing images of Kannon. The number is significant because in the *Lotus Sutra*, Kannon declares she will take 33 different forms to save anyone in distress. This pilgrimage begins at Nachi-san in Wakayama prefecture and continues in a circuitous route ending east of Lake Biwa.

There are other short "walks" between temples and shrines devoted to the Seven Deities of Good Fortune (*shichifukujin meguri*). In Tokyo, one popular walking course is in the Nihonbashi area and includes *Suitengu*.

◼ Why is one form of drawing lots called *Amida-kuji*?

Japanese people sometimes choose a winner or a prize by a form of lottery. One person draws a **lattice pattern** on paper. Each participant traces a line across the pattern to determine who wins. The pattern looks like the **circle of brightness** surrounding the Buddha Amida. So this kind of *kuji–biki* (drawing lots) is called *Amida-kuji*. Drawing lots like this is a way of saying that **one will leave the choice up to the buddhas and gods**.

◘ なぜ大晦日の夜に鐘を108回鳴らすのですか？

新年が明けようとする頃、寺院の鐘が打ち鳴らされ**行く年来る年**を告げます。仏教徒の人たちによると、人間には「煩悩(ぼんのう)」というものが108あり、それらは鐘を108回鳴らすことによって一つずつ祓(はら)われていくのだということです。この「大晦日の夜に鳴る鐘」は「除夜の鐘」と呼ばれています。

◉ Why do people ring temple bells 108 times on New Year's Eve?

Beginning on New Year's Eve, temple bells are rung to announce the **passing of the old year and the coming of the new.** Buddhists believe that there are 108 earthly desires or passions, *bonno*, and that by ringing the bell 108 times, one desire is dispelled each time. These "New Year's Eve bells" are called *joya no kane*.

Christianity in Japan

日本のキリスト教

■誰が、いつキリスト教を日本にもたらしたのですか?

フランシスコ・ザビエル(1506-1552)はキリスト教を広めるため、二人の宣教師を連れて1549年に日本へやって来ました。ザビエルはイエズス会を創設し、その修道士としても知られていました。インドとマラッカで布教をするうち、ザビエルはアンジロウという名の日本人と出会います。アンジロウが語ってくれた日本の話は、ザビエルをかの地での布教へとかきたてるものでした。

ザビエルは九州の平戸を訪れ、京都へと向かいました。天皇に拝謁して日本全土に布教をする許しを得ようとしたものの、不首尾に終わります。ザビエルは1551年に日本を去ってインドへと向かい、その翌年に亡くなりました。

平戸のザビエル記念聖堂(長崎県)

■誰が、なぜキリスト教を受け入れたのですか?

ザビエルらの布教によりキリスト教信仰は九州に広まり、特に長崎近辺において最も成果を得ました。九州の大名にはキリスト教に**改宗する者**もおり、それに従うものたちが次々と入信しました。その動機の一部にあったのは、キリスト教を受け入れることで藩に他国との貿易の道筋をつけたいというものでした。

▣ Who brought Christianity to Japan and when?

Francis Xavier (1506–52) came to Japan with two priests in 1549 in order to spread Christianity. He was the founder of the Society of Jesus, also known as the Jesuits. While spreading Christianity in India and Malacca, he met a Japanese man named Anjiro. What Anjiro told Xavier about Japan encouraged him to go there to preach Christianity.

Xavier visited Hirado in Kyushu and traveled to Kyoto. He tried to meet the emperor to get permission to preach throughout Japan, but was unsuccessful. Xavier left Japan for India in 1551 and died the next year.

▣ Who accepted Christianity and why?

Xavier and his followers were most successful in spreading Christian belief in Kyushu, especially near Nagasaki. Some of the Kyushu daimyo **converted** to Christianity and their followers joined them. Part of the motivation for accepting Christianity was that the local governments hoped that it would lead to trade with other nations.

▣キリスト教は、なぜ禁じられたのですか？

豊臣秀吉が支配する国家において、キリスト教は初めて**制限**されました。徳川幕府の統治下になると、**布教者**が日本から追放され、キリスト教は事あるごとに禁止されていました。

弾圧が始まったのは、長崎近辺の島原半島で起こった島原の乱からです。この辺りの領民は長年の貧困や重い年貢、ずっと続いている**飢饉**に苦しめられていました。**百姓一揆**が1637年に勃発し、そこに浪人たちが加わります。その一揆の先頭に立ったのは天草四郎という若者を指導者とする一団で、彼らはたまたまキリスト教徒でした。幕府は反乱軍を攻撃して原城を**包囲**し、そこでは残った者たちが必死の抵抗を続けました。1638年、反乱軍の食糧が尽きて城は落ち、**籠城**した者たちは皆処刑されました。この乱の鎮圧後、日本のキリスト教は事実上姿を消しました。

隠れキリシタンの里 天草の崎津天主堂（熊本県）

▣「隠れキリシタン」とは、どんなものですか？

1638年以後、キリスト教信者の中には地下に潜って「隠れキリシタン」になる者もありました。隠れキリシタンたちは密かに礼拝を行い、仏教徒のふりをして信仰を続けました。神父がいなかったので**一般**の信者を指導者として仰ぎ、外国の宣教師たちから教わった**典礼**や教義を**口承**で伝えていき

■ Why was Christianity banned?

Toyotomi Hideyoshi was the first national leader to **suppress** Catholic Christianity. Under the Tokugawa shogunate, **missionaries** were banned from Japan and Christianity was banned from time to time.

Serious suppression began with the Shimabara Rebellion in the Shimabara peninsula near Nagasaki. The area suffered from continuous poverty, high taxes and continuing **famine**. A **peasant rebellion** broke out in 1637, and the peasant were joined by samurai who had no employment. They were led by a young leader named Amakusa Shiro and others, who happened to be Christians. The shogunate attacked the rebels and **laid siege** to Hara Castle where the remaining rebels fought desperately. In 1638 the rebels ran out of food, the castle was captured and all of the occupants were killed. After this defeat, Christianity in Japan virtually disappeared.

■ What are "hidden Christians" (*kakure kirishitan*)?

After 1638, some Christians went underground, becoming "hidden Christians," *kakure kirishitan*. They practiced their beliefs in secret. They kept their beliefs and practices, while appearing to become Buddhists. They had no priests, so they depended on **lay** leaders. They passed on **by word of mouth** the **liturgy** and doctrines they had learned from the

ました。このような状態は、1868年に江戸時代が終わるまで続きます。

■キリスト教の禁止は、いつ解かれたのですか?

キリスト教が禁止されたままの状態は、「鎖国」が終わるまで続きました。江戸時代末期には、カトリック教会の宣教師たちが活動を**再開する**ために来日することが徐々に許されていきます。1864年には長崎の大浦にカトリックの教会（大浦天主堂）が建てられました。翌年、浦上村の百姓たちが集団でこの教会を訪れます。彼らは神父に告げました。「私どもは神父さまと心を同じくしています」、これが最初の証言となって、隠れキリシタンがまだ日本にいたことが明らかとなりました。

大浦天主堂（長崎県）

しかしながら、キリスト教**禁止令**が完全に解かれたのは1873年になってからのことでした。

■キリスト教が日本に与えた影響とは、どんなものですか?

キリスト教の宣教師たちは、小学校から大学までの一貫教育をする私立学校を設立しました。カトリック系が建てたのは上智大学（東京）と南山大学（名古屋）、プロテスタント系は同志社大学（京都）、青山学院大学（東京）、立教大学（東京）、国際基督教大学（東京）です。これらの大学の学生はほとんどがキリスト教信者ではありませんが、**礼拝**や授業などを通してキリスト教

foreign missionaries. This continued until the end of the Tokugawa period in 1868.

◼ When was Christianity permitted again?

Christianity continued to be banned until the end of the period of **national seclusion**, *sakoku*. During the last years of the Tokugawa period, Catholic missionaries were gradually allowed into Japan to **resume** activity. A Catholic church was built in the Oura section of Nagasaki in 1864. The next year a group of farmers from the village of Urakami visited the church. They announced to the priest, "Our hearts are the same as yours." This was the first evidence that so-called "hidden Christians" (*kakure kirishitan*), existed in Japan.

However, it was not until 1873 that the **ban** on Christianity was completely lifted.

◼ What impact has Christianity had on Japan?

Christian missions established private schools from elementary through university levels. The Catholics established the universities now called Sophia University (Tokyo) and Nanzan University (Nagoya). Protestant groups established Doshisha University (Kyoto), Aoyama Gakuin University (Tokyo), Rikkyo University (Tokyo) and International Christian University (Tokyo). Few of the students at these universities

の信仰に触れることとなります。日本政府の統計によると、日本人口の約2.5%がキリスト教徒だということです。

■キリスト教式の結婚式を挙げる日本人がいるのはなぜですか？

ある調査によると、2000年に日本で結婚した人たちの50%が「キリスト教」式だったということです。これにはホテル内の「チャペル」において本当の「**牧師**」でない人によって執り行われた結婚式も含まれています。事前の結婚カウンセリングは一切なく、カップルが教会に通うこともありません。

それ以外の結婚式は、ほとんどすべてが神前式です。

are Christian, but they are exposed to Christian beliefs through **chapel services** and regular classes. According to Japanese government statistics, about 2.5% of the Japanese population is Christian.

◘ Why do some Japanese have Christian weddings?

One survey says that in 2000 almost 50% of all weddings in Japan were "Christian" in style. This includes weddings at "chapels" in hotels where a person who is not a real "**minister**" performs the ceremonies. There is no marital counseling beforehand and the couple do not attend church.

The other weddings are almost all Shinto in form.

New Religions and
New-New Religions

新興宗教と新新興宗教

■いわゆる「新興宗教」とはどんなものですか？

戦後の混乱期に出現した新しい宗教は「新興宗教」と呼ばれるようになり、戦後憲法によって保障された信教の自由の下、その多くが大いに**栄え**ました。新しい規定では**宗教組織**に完全な**自治権**が与えられ、政府の役割はそういった組織を**正規**の宗教団体として登録することのみでした。いったん正式に登録されるとそれらの**団体は納税免除**の対象となり、この恩恵によって次々と新興宗教が生まれました。

こうした団体の多くが、**先祖供養**と現世利益（げんせりやく）と特定の経典重視を混ぜ合わせたようなものを主旨としていました。中には教義や、あるいは聖書のようなものさえ必要とせず、信者となりそうな人に何かしらの利益や救いの約束などを与えるのみの団体もありました。従来からある教典で最もよく**再解釈**に用いられたものの一つが妙法蓮華経です。これを信奉している団体の多くはもっぱら**素人**のみで成り立っており、つまり**正式に継承を認められた**宗派とは無関係でした。

多くの場合、カリスマ教祖というものも存在していました。それは特別な方法で崇められ、その生い立ちが何かしらの形で組織の教えを象徴するようになる人です。奇跡が起こったり、魂が癒されたりすることもカリスマ教祖のおかげだと考えられている場合もあります。

さらに新しくできた宗教団体は、時に「新新興宗教」と呼ばれます。

▣ What are the so-called "New Religions"?

The new religions that appeared during the chaos that followed World War II came to be called *shinko shukyo*, "new religions." Many **prospered** under the freedom of religion guaranteed by the postwar constitution. Under the new regulations, **religious bodies** were given complete **autonomy**. The government's only role was to register them as **legitimate** religious bodies. Once properly registered, these groups were **exempt from taxation**, a benefit that promoted a lot of new religions.

Most of these groups was a combination of **reverence for ancestors**, promise of worldly benefits and focus on a particular sutra. For some groups, it was not necessary to have doctrines or even sacred scriptures but only to offer potential members some sort of benefit or the promise of salvation. Among the most common of the traditional scriptures that were **reinterpreted** was the *Lotus Sutra*, and many of the groups that embraced this sutra consisted exclusively of **laypeople**, that is, people with no connection to an **ordained** priesthood.

In the majority of cases, there was also a charismatic or shamanistic leader, a person who is revered in a special way or a person whose life story in some way comes to symbolize the teachings of the organization. Miraculous powers and spiritual healing may also be attributed to these leaders.

Religious groups formed more recently are sometimes referred to as "New New Religions" (*shin-shinko shukyo*).

◼ 天理教とは、どんなものですか？

天理教は日本で最も大きい宗教団体の一つです。神道の一派（教派神道）として奈良県のある村で創立され、そこは現在天理市となっています。

天理教は、人々が純粋で真面目な心を育てれば陽気にくらすことができるという考えを掲げています。天理教の倫理とは、人間は悪ではないがその魂が「八つのほこり（をしい、ほしい、にくい、かわい、うらみ、はらだち、よく、こうまん）」で覆われており、これらが人間に不幸をもたらし、人間が輝くことを妨げているとするものです。「ほこり」が取り除かれれば、その人間の魂は輝きを取り戻し、救われると考えられています。

天理教は幅広い分野にわたって拡大してきました。現在運営しているものには、天理大学、病院、ラジオ局、天理図書館などがあり、図書館には国宝、重要文化財などが収蔵されています。天理教は約200万人の信者を有し、ブラジルやコンゴ、アメリカ合衆国へと広がりつつあります。

◼ 金光教とはどんなものですか？

金光教は教派神道の連合会に属する一派です。この教団では人間は皆等しいものとされ、心から天地金乃神を崇拝し、まじめに働き、他人を思いやれば、神の加護が得られると考えられています。1990年時点での教団報告によると、その信者数は約45万人でした。天理教と金光教は

◾ What is Tenrikyo?

Literally "religion of divine wisdom," Tenrikyo is one of the largest religious groups in Japan. A Shinto sect (*Kyoha Shinto*), it was founded in a village in Nara Prefecture which is now Tenri City.

It promotes the idea that a better world is possible if people simply develop a pure and simple heart. Tenrikyo ethics hold that human beings are not evil, but their souls are covered with eight kinds of dust (*yatsu no hokori*): greed, stinginess, partiality, hatred, animosity, anger, covetousness and arrogance. It is these that cause human unhappiness and prevent human beings from "shining." If these forms of "dust" are removed, the human spirit will shine once more and salvation will be achieved.

Tenrikyo has expanded widely, and it now operates Tenri University, a hospital, a radio station and Tenri Central Library, which contains a significant collection of National Treasures and Important Cultural Properties. Tenrikyo has some two million adherents and is expanding into Brazil, Congo and the United States.

◾ What is Konko-kyo?

Konko-kyo, literally "teaching of the golden light," is a syncretist sect of Shinto. The sect believes that all humans are equal and that if a person worships the deity Konjin sincerely, works industriously and is considerate of others, he or she will be blessed by the deity. As of 1990, the sect claimed some 450,000

戦後に急成長した「新興宗教」の先駆けと見なされることがあります。

◾ 大本教とは、どんなものですか？

大本教はその流れを汲む宗教団体を数多く生み出した教団であり、1892年に立教されました。

大本教の教えは現社会を批判し改革を求めるものであり、救いはエリートたちではなく庶民から始まるということを言わんとしていました。これは天皇や政府といった権力者側にとっては、革命的かつ脅威的な発想でした。天皇を頂点とするこの社会から大本教を排除しなければ、政府は抑圧を強いられることになります。なぜなら大本教が、天皇ではなく「神」がこの世を平和で友愛溢れるものに創り変えると言っていたからです。戦後、大本教は信者数が大幅に減少しました。

◾ PL教団とは、どんなものですか？

パーフェクト リバティー教団、通称PL教団は1946年に立教されました。教団名は「完全なる自由」という意味です。PL教団は「人生は芸術である」という真理の下に「芸術生活」を理想に掲げており、幸せと充実感は日常生活の中で自らの個性を思う存分に発揮し、ひいては人のため社会のためになることによって生じると考えています。

members. Tenrikyo and Konkokyo are sometimes seen as the forerunners of the "new religions" that sprang up after the Second World War.

◼ What is Omoto-kyo?

Omoto-kyo, literally "teaching of the great origin," was established in 1892. It is the parent of a large number of separate religious organizations.

Omoto-kyo teachings criticized contemporary society and called for reform. Its message was that salvation began not with the elite but with the common people. This was an idea which seemed both revolutionary and menacing to the authority of the Emperor and the government. While Omoto-kyo did not reject the imperial system, the organization was suppressed because it said that a *kami* other than the emperor would transform the world into one of peace and brotherhood. After World War II, Omoto-kyo membership declined significantly.

◼ What is PL Kyodan?

PL Kyodan, the Church of Perfect Liberty, was founded in 1946. The name comes from English: "Perfect Liberty." Based on the idea that "Life is Art," the group holds "the artistic life" as its ideal. Happiness and satisfaction will result when the individual expresses his or her personality perfectly in every way—in the interest of other people and society as a whole.

教団本部は大阪郊外の富田林市に所在しており、本部施設の周りにはゴルフ場、病院、小学校、中学校、高等学校（野球で有名なPL学園）、専門学校などがあります。

◾️生長の家とは、どんなものですか？

生長の家は1929年に創立された一宗派です。この教団は人と神との結び付き、そして「生命の実相」を悟るための努力精進を強調しており、これを実現することで幸福が現れ、病や貧困に打ち勝つことができると断言しています。その折衷的な見解においてはキリスト教も、仏教も、神道も、他すべての正しい宗教は実質的に同一あり、これに従って信徒は自由に他の宗教へも入信することができます。他宗派に対しては、その団体から害されることがない限り対抗姿勢を見せることはありません。日本政府はこの宗派を「その他の宗教」として分類しています。生長の家もまた、海外での布教活動に力を入れてきています。

◾️霊友会とは、どんなものですか？

霊友会は日本で最も大きな在家教団の一つであり、どの仏教宗派とも直接のつながりはありません。

その教えは先祖供養、家系、法華経に基づく仏の戒（いまし）めを強調しています。霊友会の考え方

The organization's headquarters are in Tonda-bayashi, on the outskirts of Osaka. Surrounding this building are a golf course, a hospital, an elementary school, a middle school, a high school (PL Gakuen) which is known for its baseball team, and a finishing school.

◼ What is Seicho no Ie?

Seicho no Ie, House of Growth, is a religious sect founded in 1929. It stresses man's relationship with the divine and the individual's efforts to realize "the truth of life." This realization promises happiness and victory over both illness and poverty. In its eclectic viewpoint, the teachings of Christianity, Buddhism, Shinto and all other true religions are actually one and the same. In line with this, members are free to become members of other religions, too. The group shows no resistance to other religions, unless that other group requires that people suffer. The sect is classified by the Japanese government among "other religions." Seicho no Ie has also stressed proselytizing overseas.

◼ What is Reiyukai?

Reiyukai, Spiritual-Friends-Association, is one of the largest lay religious organizations in Japan. The group has no direct affiliation with any Buddhist sect.

The teachings of Reiyukai stress veneration of ancestors, the family system and the Buddhist tradition

は独創的で、先祖供養をすること、かつてのように父方母方両家を家系とすること、一般的倫理観を持つことこそが社会調和の鍵だとし、この世で救われるか否かは真心をこめて先祖の霊を供養することにかかっていると見なしています。この団体の中心となる活動に「法座」と呼ばれる座談会があり、そこでは在家の指導者が信徒たちの個人的な相談に乗ったり、宗教的な教育を施したりします。

■創価学会とは、どんなものですか？

1930年に創立された創価学会は、仏教宗派の日蓮正宗から独立した在家信徒団体です。その目標には、日蓮の教えに基づいた社会改革というものがあります。

創価学会はすべての人間が仏性を持っていると見なしており、信、行、学、が必要にして不可欠であると説いています。信とはは「南無妙法蓮華経」（私は妙法蓮華経に帰依します）という題目を唱え、法華経を読誦(どくじゅ)することです。行とは仏教徒として日常的に精進することであり、その主軸たるものが日蓮正宗の宣伝です。この修行のことを「折伏(しゃくぶく)」といい、積極的な布教を意味します。学とは日蓮の教えを学ぶことを指しています。この宗派は、創価学会と日蓮正宗のみが日蓮の見出した真実を正確に伝えていると主張しており、この教えから外れるすべての宗教行為は異端と見なされ、避けられます。会員はいかなる神道行事にも参加しないものとされ、初

based in the *Lotus Sutra*. Reiyukai originally saw veneration of ancestors and a revival of the extended family and traditional morality as the keys to social harmony. The possibility of salvation in this world was seen as grounded in faithful veneration of ancestral spirits. Among the important practices of the group is the group meeting called *hoza*, literally "Dharma circle," in which a lay leader counsels members on personal problems and offers religious instruction.

▣ What is Soka Gakkai?

Founded in 1930, Soka Gakkai is an independent lay organization of the Nichiren Shoshu sect of Buddhism. Its aims include a reform of society based on the teachings of Nichiren.

Assuming that all human beings possess buddha-nature, Soka Gakkai teaches that faith, practice and study are essentials. The first is the chanting of "*Namu Myoho Renge-kyo*" (I believe in the Lotus Sutra) and reciting the sutra. The second is including Buddhist activities into daily life, the key element of which is propagating the teachings of Nichiren Shoshu. Characteristic of this aspect is *shakubuku*, aggressive propagation. The third refers to studying the teachings of Nichiren. The sect claims that only Soka Gakkai and Nichiren Shoshu represent accurately the truth discovered by Nichiren. All religious activities outside this tradition are to be considered as heresy and are to be avoided. Members are not supposed to participate

詣でや祭りなどには行くことはありません。

創価学会は独自の大学（創価大学）を運営し、日刊誌（聖教新聞）を発行し、数々の文化および社会活動を主催しています。公明党という本格的な政党を1964年に結成しましたが、1970年にはその政党から分離しました。

◼ 立正佼成会とは、どんなものですか？

立正佼成会は日本で最大規模に入る在家仏教信徒団体です。創立は1938年であり、伝統的な日蓮宗の教えと法華経に基づく新宗教の一つですが、日蓮宗派との正式な関係は一切ありません。

立正佼成会は法華経を一般人にも理解し易いものとすることに力を入れ、この宇宙では人や物すべてが相互に依存していると強調し、総合的には先祖供養を奨励しています。

その活動の中には「法座」への参加があり、少人数での座談会で内省をしたり、個人的な相談をしたり、グループ長からの教育を受けたりします。この方法の効果はすでに現れており、会員たちが互いに引き止めあって信者を続けたり、新規の会員を呼び込んだりしています。立正佼成会もまた世界的な宗教協力と平和の促進活動で知られています。特に庭野平和賞を設定していることは有名で、その賞を通じてめざましい

in any Shinto activities such as shrine visits at the New Year or in festivals.

Soka Gakkai has its own university (Soka University), daily newspaper (*Seikyo Shimbun*) and cultural and social programs. In 1964 it founded a full-fledged political party, Komeito (Clean Government Party), but separated from the party in 1970.

◼ What is Rissho Koseikai?

Rissho Koseikai (Society for the Establishment of Righteousness and Personal Perfection through Fellowship) is one of the largest organizations of lay Buddhists in Japan. Founded in 1938, it is one of the new religions based on Nichiren tradition and the *Lotus Sutra*, but it has no formal relation with a Nichiren sect.

It emphasizes making the *Lotus Sutra* easy for laypeople to understand, emphasizes the interdependence of all human beings and all things in the universe and therefore encourages the veneration of ancestors.

Among the central activities is participation in *hoza*, small groups aimed at self-reflection and personal counseling and instruction by a group leader. This method has proved effective in keeping members involved with one another and in attracting new members. Rissho Koseikai is also known for its ecumenical cooperation and promotion of world peace, especially through the Niwano Peace Prize, which is awarded to remarkable religious leaders or groups that

活躍をした宗教指導者や、あるいは宗教間の対話、人権保護、紛争の解決などに貢献した団体などを表彰しています。

◉阿含宗とは、どんなものですか?

この「新新興宗教」は1978年に創立されたもので、「護摩」という壮大な火の儀式によって少なからぬマスコミの注目を集めています。教団は不幸な死霊の「祟り」が生者に災いすると主張しており、これらの悪霊は護摩を通して良い霊へと転化され、その場にいる人々に恩恵をもたらすと考えています。

阿含宗に関して最も知られているものが「星まつり」であり、京都の中心部を遠く離れた場所で毎年2月11日に行われます。その日は折しも建国記念日であり、マスコミに広く報じられることもあって、結果的に50万人超の観客が動員されます。そんな中で行われる星まつりは、燃え盛る二つの大きな薪(たきぎ)の山を中心に進行し、その上に願い事などが書かれた護摩木が積み上げられます。この時、ちょうどいい頃合を見計らってその場にいる人たちに出番が与えられ、世界の平和を、幸福を、先祖の救いなどを祈願できるようになっています。

◉オウム真理教(アーレフ)とは、どんなものですか?

1987年、オウム真理教は松本智津夫(1955–)

contribute to dialogue between religions, protection of human rights and the resolution of conflict.

◼ What is Agon-shu?

This "new-new religion," founded in 1978, gathers considerable media attention as a result of its spectacular fire rites, *goma*. The group claims that unhappy spirits of the dead affect the living by causing spiritual hindrances and *tatari* (pollution). Through its fire rites, these afflicting spirits are believed to be transformed into benevolent spirits that bestow benefits on participants.

Its most well-known feature is its *hoshi matsuri*, or star festival, held annually outside Kyoto on February 11. That day happens to be National Foundation Day. Widely advertised in the media—and as a result attended by over half a million visitors—this outdoor ritual centers on the burning of two huge pyres of branches upon which are piled wooden sticks inscribed with requests are written. The occasion is carefully orchestrated to give attendees an opportunity to express their hopes for world peace, for happiness and the salvation of their ancestors.

◼ What is Aum Shinrikyo (Aleph)?

Aum Shinrikyo was founded by Matsumoto Chizuo

によって設立されました。松本は麻原彰晃と改名します。元阿含宗信者だった麻原はヨーガや仙道（せんどう）、そして黙示録的（もくしろく）予言などにのめり込んでいきました。1995年3月20日、オウム真理教の信者たちが東京の地下鉄車内5ヵ所に神経ガスのサリンを撒布し、12名を死に至らせ、5500名以上を負傷させました。その後続いた捜査によって教団の他の犯罪への関与が明らかとなり、その中には疑惑のあった数々の殺人や批判者へのガス攻撃なども含まれていました。

　麻原らは逮捕され裁判にかけられました。その間、教団は名前をアーレフと改めます。世間を震撼させたサリン事件は、日本に新興宗教への少なからぬ懸念を生みました。

■白光真宏会とは、どんなものですか？

　白光真宏会について最もよく知られているのは、いろいろな国の言語による「世界人類が平和でありますように」の言葉が表示されたポールを立てていることです。この団体の儀式では、個人の幸福を、そして世界の平和を祈ります。白光真宏会とは、日本を白光の核として、そこから世界中に平和が広がっていくことを表現した名前です。

(1955-) in 1987. He changed his name to Asahara Shoko. Formerly a member of Agon-shu, he became involved in yoga, esoteric spiritualism, and apocalyptic prophecies. On March 20, 1995, members of Aum Shinrikyo released sarin nerve gas on five Tokyo subway cars, killing 12 people and injuring more than 5,500. Subsequent investigations tied the group to other crimes, including alleged murders and gas attacks on critics.

Asahara and other members were arrested and stood trial. In the meantime, the group changed its name to Aleph. The sensational sarin attack has created considerable concern in Japan regarding new religious sects.

▣ What is Byakko Shinkokai?

This group is best known for erecting "peace poles" that have the words "May Peace Prevail on Earth" written in the local language. The group incorporates prayers for the individual and for world peace in its rituals. It portrays Japan as the holy core from which peace will spread throughout the world.

Ceremonies and social customs
(semi-religious, cross-religion)

宗教的意味合いを含む儀式と社会の風習

◼ 年中行事

お正月：この言い方は新年における始めの何日間かを表すものであり、最初の日だけを指す場合は「元旦」といいます。お正月には多くの日本人が寺社に**足を運び**ますが、これは「初詣で」と呼ばれています。

初詣で：「初詣で」とは、年明けの時期に神社仏閣へ最初の参拝をすることを指していうものです。こうした参拝は日本各地で見られ、たいていは大晦日の深夜から始まって正月三ヵ日の間続きます。この期間中、初詣でランキングの上位5ヵ所にはそれぞれ数百万の人出があります。5ヵ所中3つが神社で2つがお寺であり、月並みに人気の順で挙げると、明治神宮（東京）、新勝寺（成田）、川崎大師（川崎）、伏見稲荷大社（京都）、鶴岡八幡宮（鎌倉）となっています。その他人気があるのは、東京の浅草寺（浅草観音）、京都の八坂神社などです。

どんと祭：1月15日頃に開かれるいくつもの火祭です。これらの祭りでは正月飾りや神社の飾り、お守りやお札などが**焚き火**で燃やされ、点火の際には無病息災と豊作が祈願されます。主なものは仙台の大崎八幡宮におけるどんと祭であり、市内から神社をめざして歩く「裸参り」と1月14日の夜を照らす焚き火を呼び物としています。

◘ Annual events

O-shogatsu: This expression refers to the first days of the New Year, while the term for just New Years Day is *gantan*. During the first few days of the year, many Japanese **pay a visit** to a shrine or temple, which is called *hatsumode*.

Hatsumode: The expression *hatsumode* refers to a person's first visit to a Shinto shrine or a Buddhist temple during the New Year period. These visits are a national phenomenon and usually take place between midnight on New Year's Eve and the first three days of the year. During this period, several million people visit each of the top five religious sites, three of which are Shinto shrines and two of which are Buddhist temples. In the usual order of popularity, these are: Meiji Shrine (Tokyo), Narita-san (Shinshoji) Temple (Narita), Kawasaki Daishi Temple (Kawasaki), Fushimi Inari Shrine (Kyoto) and Tsurugaoka Hachiman Shrine (Kamakura). Other popular places to visit are Sensoji (Asakusa Kannon) in Tokyo and Yasaka Shrine in Kyoto.

Donto-sai: Fire Festivals held around January 15. At these festivals, Shinto decorations, shrine ornaments and talismans are gathered and burned in **bonfires**. These are set on fire to wish for good health and a rich harvest. A major example is the Donto-sai at Osaki Hachiman-gu in Sendai, which features a "naked" pilgrimage through the city streets to the shrine and the lighting of the bonfire on the night of January 14.

節分：鬼を**追い払う**ための伝統的な儀式であり、**旧暦**で冬が終わる2月3日に行われます。この日の晩には災厄をもたらす鬼が出ると信じられていたため、きまって家庭では家の内外に**豆をまき**（「豆まき」）立春前夜に出てくるという鬼を一匹残らず追い散らそうとしていました。今日の人たちは「鬼は外！　福は内！」と大声で繰り返しつつ、なんだか遊びながら豆まきをしているようにも見えます。成田山の新勝寺のような大寺院では、横綱や人気タレントなどの有名人が舞台の上から見物人たちに向けて豆をまき、その豆は**縁起物**として持ち帰れます。

流し雛

桃の節句：3月3日の「桃の節句」は、より一般的には「雛祭」として知られています。現代の雛祭にはいくつかの起源が存在します。平安時代、宮廷人が**陰陽師**に自分の**穢**れを祓わせる際には、紙の人形にその穢れが移されて川や海などに流されていました。つまり、雛祭は一種の**お祓い**でした。江戸時代、これは平安時代の別の風習である女の子の紙人形遊びと合わさり、家に雛壇を作ってお雛さまを飾ることへと発展していきました。

お彼岸：春分または秋分、およびその前後3日間を合わせた7日の期間のことで、「彼岸会」とも呼ばれます。仏様のいる家族はお寺で説教を聴いたり、お経を上げたりすることもあります

Setsubun: A traditional ceremony to **dispel** demons, held on February 3, the last day of winter by the **lunar calendar**. It was believed that demons bringing misfortune appeared in the evening, so families would **scatter beans** (*mamemaki*) inside and outside their houses and other buildings to scatter any demons that might appear on the night before the traditional beginning of spring. People today may do this partly in play, while chanting "*Oni wa soto! Fuku wa uchi!*" ("Out with demons! In with good fortune!") At major shrines such as Narita's Shinshoji, *sumo* Grand Champions, movie and television stars, and other celebrities scatter beans from raised platforms into crowds that are assembled for the event. The people collect the beans as **good luck charms**.

Momo no sekku: The "Peach Festival" on March 3 is more commonly known as *hina matsuri*, the Doll Festival. There are several sources for the modern Doll Festival. During the Heian period, courtiers had **diviners** remove their impurities by having the impurities transferred to paper images, which were cast into a river or the ocean. In other words, it was a kind of **exorcism**. In the Edo period, this custom merged with another Heian custom of girls playing with paper dolls and evolved into displaying dolls of courtiers and attendants on tiers set up in the home.

Higan: A seven-day period—the vernal or autumnal equinox with the three days preceding and following—this is also called *higan-e*. Believers may attend lectures or sutra readings at temples, and most

が、たいていの人は先祖の墓参りをします。「彼岸」とは「向こう岸」にある極楽浄土のことで、信者たちは自身が悟りに達するため、そして先祖の**供養をする**ために、この期間に特別な行を修めるものとされています。

花祭：花祭は4月8日に行われる年中行事であり、釈迦の誕生を祝うものです。仏教の世界には釈迦が生まれた時に甘露の雨が降り注いだという言い伝えがあり、そのことからお寺に小さな誕生仏の像が安置され、参拝者がそれに「甘茶」をかけるようになっています。この行事の法要としての名前を「**灌仏会**」、または「**降誕会**」といいます。

端午の節句：　5月5日はこどもの日ですが、もとは伝統的な年中行事を行う五節句の一つとされていました。それが男の子を祝う日となり、同様に3月3日が女の子を祝う雛祭となりました。戦後に5月5日は休日とされ、新たに「こどもの日」と名付けられましたが、今日でも男の子の節句祝いが行われています。

七夕：「五節句」と呼ばれるものの一つであり、（旧暦に合わせて）7月7日、または（新暦に合わせて）8月7日に行われます。中国の民間伝承が日本に伝わり、この地に元からあった棚機津女の伝説と合わさって七夕が生まれました。それは朝廷で執り行う年中行事の一つとなり、お盆に近いことから先祖の霊を迎えるための行事に結び付けられるようになりました。しかしながら現代における七夕とは、おおむね**短冊**に願い

visit the graves of their ancestors. *Higan* is "the other shore," the ideal Pure Land, and believers are supposed to make special efforts during this period to achieve enlightenment themselves and **venerate** their ancestors.

Hana matsuri: The Flower Festival is an annual festival held on April 8 to celebrate the birth of Shakyamuni. Buddhist tradition says that when the Buddha was born, sweet nectar poured down like rain. Consequently, temples set up small images of Buddha as a child, and over it visitors pour *amacha*, **hydrangea tea**. The Buddhist name for the event is *Kanbutsu-e* or *Kotan-e*.

Tango no sekku: May 5, Children's Day, originated as one of five traditional celebrations held through the year. It became a festival for boys, corresponding to the Doll Festival for girls on March 3. After World War II, it was made a national holiday and renamed Children's Day, but even today it celebrates boys.

Tanabata: One of the traditional five festivals, called *gosekku*, held either on July 7 (in accord with the old calendar) or August 7 (in accord with the new calendar). Originating in Chinese folk legend, in Japan it merged with native legends of a celestial weaver maiden who was believed to weave clothing for the gods. The festival became one of the annual events observed by the imperial court. Due to the fact that it fell close to the *O-bon* festival, it became associ-

事を書いて竹の枝に吊るすといった内容のものです。

盂蘭盆会：この仏教行事は先祖の霊を敬うためのものであり、「盂蘭盆」、もしくは「お盆」としても知られています。従来は7月13日から15日にかけて行われていましたが、現在は地域によって8月中旬をその期間とするところもあります。

伝統的なお盆には、故人の魂を迎えるための「盆棚(しつら)」が仏壇の前に設えられ、僧が呼ばれてお経を上げます。先祖の墓はきれいに掃除され、13日には先祖が迷わずたどり着けるように出迎えの火などが外に灯されます。16日には、同様にして先祖を送り出すための灯りが置かれます。土地によっては、先祖の送り出しに提灯が川や海に流されるところもあります。

地域の人たちが集まって踊る「盆踊り」は、**自治会**が主催してお寺などの場所で開かれます。これは帰ってきた死者の魂を喜ばせるためのものですが、生者が楽しむためのものでもあります。

「お盆」と「お正月」は日本における年中の二大行事であり、共通の特徴を持っています。お盆とお正月はまた、普段は離れて暮らしている家族が一堂に会する年に二回の時でもあります。

祭り：祭りは年間を通して行われるものです

ated with welcoming the spirits of the ancestors. The modern Tanabata, however, involves mostly writing wishes on paper strips that are hung on branches of bamboo.

Urabon'e: Also known as *Urabon* or *O-bon*, this Buddhist observance of respecting the spirits of ancestors was traditionally held from July 13 to 15, but in some regions it is now observed in mid-August.

Traditionally a "spirit altar" is set up before the family Buddhist altar to welcome the souls of the departed, then a priest is asked to come and read a sutra. The ancestors' graves are cleaned and welcoming fires or lanterns are put out on the 13th to help the ancestors find their way. On the 16th, similar lights are placed for sending off the ancestors. In some places, lanterns are floated out onto a river or onto the ocean to send off the ancestors.

Bon odori, community dances, are held at temples and by **local community associations**. While intended to please and entertain the spirits of the returning dead, they are also for the entertainment of the living.

O-bon and *O-shogatsu* are the two major festivals of the year in Japan and share common characteristics. They are also the two times a year when family members gather together from wherever they live.

Matsuri: There are festivals all through the year,

が、各地の神社で祭りが盛んな時期を一つ挙げるなら10月中旬です。こうした祭りでは、たいてい地元の人々が「**神輿**（みこし）」をかついで神社の周辺一帯を回ります。神輿のかつぎ手はたいてい男性であり、しっかりと協力し合うことが必要とされます。それは見ている人に、皆一丸となって地域のためにがんばろうという気持ちを思い起こさせるものです。

七五三：11月15日の七五三には、三歳および七歳の女の子と三歳および五歳の男の子が神社などに参拝します。どの子も新しい衣装に身を包んで、健やかな成長を祈ります。

除夜の鐘：毎年、「大晦日」の終わりから年明けにかけて寺院の鐘が打ち鳴らされ、行く年来る年を告げます。仏教には、人間は108つの「煩悩」に苦しむという考え方があり、除夜の鐘が108回鳴らされ、一回鳴る毎に煩悩が一つ祓われるとされています。

■日本人が忌み嫌うものとは、どんなものですか？

不吉とされている番号には「死」の**同音異義語**である「4」、そして「苦」のそれである「9」などがあります。例えば、病院の診察室といった場所にはこれらを外した番号が振られ、近代的なマンションなどの建物でさえ、各階にこうした番号の部屋がない場合があります。

but one of the peak periods for local shrine festivals is mid-October. These usually involve the carrying of a *mikoshi*, a **portable shrine**, around the neighborhood of the shrine by people from the local community. Carrying the *mikoshi* requires that the carriers—usually men—cooperate closely, a symbolic reminder that the community should work together in harmony to achieve the common good.

Shichi-go-san: Girls of three and seven and boys of three and five years of age visit a shrine at the *Shichi-go-san* (literally "7–5–3") festival on November 15. They dress in new clothes and pray for a safe and healthy future.

Joya no kane: Each year, beginning on New Year's Eve (*Omisoka*), and continuing into New Year's Day, bells at Buddhist temples are rung to announce the passing of the old year and the arrival of the new. Buddhism holds that humans suffer from 108 passions (*bonno*). The bells are rung 108 times, each ring destroying one of the desires.

▣ What taboos do Japanese follow?

Inauspicious numbers include the number 4 (*shi*), which is a **homonym** for death (*shi*), and the number 9 (*ku*), which is a homonym for suffering and pain (*ku*). For example, hospital consultation rooms will skip these numbers. Even modern apartment buildings may skip these numbers for the rooms on each floor.

結婚披露宴などのスピーチでは、帰る、戻る、切るといった言葉は避けられます。

むかしはずっと出産や月経や死が忌み嫌われていました。このため、子どもを生んだばかりの女性はたとえお宮参りの時であっても神社に行くことはなく、代わりに子どもは父親と祖母が連れて参拝していました。

■ 仏教で禁じられている食べ物には、どんなものがありますか？

大昔の日本では仏教で動物の殺生が禁じられ、とりわけ四足（よつあし）は良くないとされていました。「鯨」を食べることが良しとされていたのは、それが魚と見なされていたからです。山間部では、「猪」を「山鯨」とすることでこれを回避しました。

■ 「六曜」とはどんなものですか？

「六曜」とは、その日の吉凶（きっきょう）を表す6種類の事項であり、6日間を一巡として決まった順番で繰り返されます。六曜は中国から持ち込まれ、日本において江戸時代の中頃から実際に用いられました。日本のカレンダーには、今でも六曜が印刷されたものがあります。

六曜の日取りは以下の順に従います。

先勝──午前は吉、午後は凶

友引──正午のみ吉

先負──午後は吉

In speeches at wedding parties, words such as *kaeru* (return), *modoru* (go back home), and *kiru* (separate, cut) are avoided.

Traditional taboos surrounded birth, menstruation and death. Because of these, women who had just given birth did not visit shrines, even to ask for the blessing of the deity. Instead, the father and grandmother took the child.

▣ What foods were taboo according to Buddhism?

In ancient Japan, Buddhism prohibited taking the life of animals, especially four-legged animals. The eating of whale (*kujira*) was acceptable because whales were categorized as fish. In mountain areas, people avoided the taboo by treating wild boar (*inoshishi*) as "mountain whales" (*yama kujira*).

▣ What are the *rokuyo*?

Rokuyo is "a system of a repeating six-day series of lucky and unlucky days." The custom was imported from China and was practiced in Japan from the mid-Tokugawa period. These designations of lucky and unlucky days are still printed on some calendars in Japan.

The six designations follow this order:
sensho—morning is lucky, afternoon is unlucky
tomobiki—only noontime is lucky
sembu—afternoon is lucky

仏滅——最も凶の日
大安——最も吉の日
赤口——正午のみ吉、前後は凶

今日の日本人は、たいていふつうのことに関しては六曜を気に掛けることはありません。ところがお宮参りや結婚などのお祝いとなると、その日が「大安」となるような日取りにすることがあります。商売を始めたり、結婚式を挙げたりする際には「仏滅」を避け、また葬式を「友引」の日にすることも敬遠します。ちなみに、この日は「友を引く」ので結婚式には良い日です。六曜を用いる慣習は**なくなりつつあります**が、地方ではまだ根強く残っています。大勢の親戚が集まる冠婚葬祭（かんこんそうさい）などは、いつも吉となるような日取りがされますが、そうしないと反対者が出てしまうためです。

■「十二支」とはどんなものですか？

日本人が取り入れた年月日の記録法および一日の分割法は中国の方式であり、その方式の完全な一周期は60種類の数詞から成るものでした。現在の日本人は毎年順番に廻ってくる十二支にしか注目していません。十二支にはそれぞれ守護仏というものが存在しています。

十二支の順番は、西暦の年に対応させると次の通りです。

子（ね）　2020年
丑（うし）　2021年

butsumetsu—the most unlucky day
taian—the most lucky day
shakko—unlucky, except for noontime

Japanese today usually do not pay any attention to these designations for ordinary events. However, they may schedule a visit to a shrine, a wedding or other celebration on a day that is *taian* (great peace). They will avoid opening a business or holding a wedding on a day that is *butsumetsu*, "Buddha's death." They will also avoid having a funeral on a day that is *tomobiki*, literally "bringing a friend." That day is a good one for a wedding. This custom is **dying out**, but it is still strong in the countryside. Any major life event that involves large groups of relatives will probably be set on a day considered fortunate, to avoid social disapproval.

◼ What are the animals of the Chinese zodiac (*junishi*)?

The Japanese adopted the Chinese system for counting days, months and years as well as the divisions of the day. The complete cycle was 60 sets of symbols. Today Japanese pay attention only to the 12 animals that come in a cycle. There is a guardian buddha or bodhisattva for each year.

The order of the animals in the zodiac, with the year according to the Western calendar, is as follows:

Rat	2020
Ox	2021

寅(とら) 2022年
卯(う) 2023年
辰(たつ) 2024年
巳(み) 2025年
午(うま) 2026年
未(ひつじ) 2027年
申(さる) 2028年
酉(とり) 2029年
戌(いぬ) 2030年
亥(い) 2031年

中国人と同じく日本人も、人はそれぞれ生まれた年の干支と似た性格を持っていると考えています。例えば亥年生まれは猪突猛進の傾向がある、つまり強気で融通の利かない人が多いとされています。最近はこのようなことを本気で信じている人はほとんどいません。

とはいうものの、ほぼすべての日本人はその年の干支を知っています。今でも年賀状、お守り、神社やお寺で売られている「絵馬」などにはその年の干支が用いられています。

■「流鏑馬」とはどんなものですか?

「流鏑馬」は平安時代(794–1185)に始められたものであり、もとは占いの一形式とされていました。馬に乗った射手が一人ずつまっすぐな馬場を疾走し、その間に三つの的を目がけて矢を放ちます。

Tiger	2022
Rabbit	2023
Dragon	2024
Snake	2025
Horse	2026
Sheep	2027
Monkey	2028
Rooster	2029
Dog	2030
Boar	2031

Like the Chinese, Japanese believed that people born in each of these years took on the character of the animal of the birth year. For example, those born in the Year of the Boar tended to run at top speed straight ahead. In other words, they tended to have strong opinions and to be **inflexible**. Few Japanese really believe such things nowadays.

However, almost all Japanese know what sign the current year is. The current year's animal is still used on New Year's greeting cards, amulets and the *ema* sold at shrines and temples.

◘ What is *yabusame*?

Called "mounted archery," *yabusame* dates from the Heian period (794–1185). It originated as a form of **divination**. Each rider shoots at three targets as his horse races down a straight track.

■「パワースポット」とは、どんなものですか?

2010年頃から、いろいろな場所を信奉する人たちが出てきました。彼らは自力でなし得ないことを可能とする「パワー」をそこで得ると信じています。「パワースポット」としてテレビや雑誌で特集されると、そこには巡礼者が訪れるようになり、特定の神社や特異な地形、木、岩、像などが崇拝の対象とされます。この現象は新しい形の精霊崇拝のようなものかもしれず、あるいは自ら努力するよりも幸運を頼む人が増えたことの表れなのかもしれません。

◘ What are "power spots"?

Beginning around 2010, some people began to place faith in places where they believe they get "power" to achieve difficult goals. Featured on TV and in magazines as "power spots," they become sites of pilgrimage. Sites include certain shrines, unique natural locales, trees, rocks and statues. This belief may be a new form of spiritualism or animism. Or it may result from an increase in the number of people who believe in luck rather than in making an effort.

付録:日本の仏教宗派

真言宗および天台宗(日本初期仏教)

真言宗	宗　　祖:空海(弘法大師) 主な寺院:高野山(金剛峰寺) 中心とされる仏:大日如来 中心とされるもの:密教、曼荼羅
天台宗	宗　　祖:最澄(伝教大師) 主な寺院:比叡山(延暦寺) 中心とされる経典:妙法蓮華経 中心とされるもの:多くの魂の救済

日本中世仏教(鎌倉仏教)

浄土教	**浄土宗** 　宗　　祖:法然 　主な修行:念仏 　中心とされるもの:阿弥陀如来への帰依
	浄土真宗 　宗　　祖:親鸞 　主な修行:念仏 　中心とされるもの:阿弥陀如来への絶対的帰依
日蓮宗	宗　　祖:日蓮 主な修行:題目を繰り返し唱えること 中心とされるもの:妙法蓮華経および日蓮大菩薩 　　　　　　　　　への帰依
禅	**臨済宗** 　宗　　祖:栄西 　主な修行:座禅、考案 　中心とされるもの:座禅および考案
	曹洞宗 　宗　　祖:道元 　主な修行:座禅 　中心とされるもの:座禅

Appendix: The Buddhist Sect of Japan

Shingon and Tendai Sects (Early Japanese Buddhism)

Shingon	Founder: Kukai (Kobo Daishi) Main temple: Mt. Koya Main image: Maha Vairocana (Dainichi) Focus: Esoteric teachings, mandala
Tendai	Founder: Saicho (Dengyo Daishi) Main temple: Enryakuji on Mt. Hiei Main scripture: *Lotus Sutra* Focus: Many paths to salvation

Medieval Buddhism (Kamakura Buddhism)

Pure Land	**Jodo** Founder: Honen Main practice: *Nembutsu* Focus: Faith in Amida
	Jodo Shin Founder: Shinran Main practice: *Nembutsu* Focus: Exclusive faith in Amida
Nichiren	Founder: Nichiren Main practice: Chanting the *daimoku* Focus: Faith in Lotus Sutra and in Nichiren as a Bodhisattva
Zen	**Rinzai** Founder: Eisai Main practice: *Zazen* (seated meditation), *koans* Focus: *Zazen* and *koans*
	Soto Founder: Dogen Main practice: *Zazen* (seated meditation) Focus: *Zazen*

Bibliography

Deal, William E. *Handbook to Life in Medieval and Early Modern Japan*. New York: Facts on File, 2006.

Inagaki, Hisao. *A Dictionary of Japanese Buddhist Terms*. Kyoto: Nagata Bunshodo, 1988.

Kasahara, Kazuo (ed.). *A History of Japanese Religion*. Tokyo: Kosei Publishing Co., 2001.

Nickoloff, Philip L. *Sacred Koyasan: A Pilgrimage to the Mountain Temple of Saint Kobo Daishi and the Great Sun Buddha*. Albany: SUNY Press, 2008.

Picken, Stuart D.B. *The A to Z of Shinto*. Lanham, MD: Scarecrow Press, 2006.

Reader, Ian. *Making Pilgrimages: Meaning and Practice in Shikoku*. Honolulu: University of Hawaii Press, 2005.

Reader, Ian. *Religion in Contemporary Japan*. Honolulu: University of Hawaii Press, 1991.

Waley, Paul. *Tokyo Now and Then: An Explorer's Guide*. New York: Weatherhill, 1984.

E-CAT

English **C**onversational **A**bility **T**est
国際英語会話力検定

● E-CATとは…
英語が話せるようになるための
テストです。インターネット
ベースで、30分であなたの発
話力をチェックします。

www.ecatexam.com

iTEP

● iTEP®とは…
世界各国の企業、政府機関、アメリカの大学
300校以上が、英語能力判定テストとして採用。
オンラインによる90分のテストで文法、リー
ディング、リスニング、ライティング、スピー
キングの5技能をスコア化。iTEP®は、留学、就
職、海外赴任などに必要な、世界に通用する英
語力を総合的に評価する画期的なテストです。

www.itepexamjapan.com

[対訳ニッポン双書]
外国人によく聞かれる日本の宗教
Japanese Religion

2011年5月10日　第1刷発行
2024年7月11日　第4刷発行

著　者　ジェームス・M・バーダマン
訳　者　澤田組

発行者　賀川　洋

発行所　IBCパブリッシング株式会社
〒162-0804 東京都新宿区中里町29番3号 菱秀神楽坂ビル
Tel. 03-3513-4511 Fax. 03-3513-4512
www.ibcpub.co.jp

印刷所　株式会社シナノパブリッシングプレス

© James M. Vardaman 2011
© IBC パブリッシング 2011
Printed in Japan

落丁本・乱丁本は、小社宛にお送りください。送料小社負担にてお取り替えいたします。
本書の無断複写(コピー) は著作権法上での例外を除き禁じられています。

ISBN978-4-7946-0076-9